ADVENTURES IN CREATING EARRINGS

D0509275

by

Laura Reid

Copyright © MCMXC by Eagle's View Publishing Company

All rights reserved. No part of this book may be reproduced or transmitted in any form or by any means, electronic or mechanical, including, but not restricted to, photocopying, recording or using any information storage or retrieval system, without permission in writing from the publisher.

Eagle's View Publishing
A WestWind, Inc. Company
6756 North Fork Road
Liberty, UT 84310

ISBN: 0-943604-28-1
Library of Congress Number: 90-82647

First Edition

Table of Contents

Acknowledgments   3
Introduction   5
Foundation Designs
    Double Point Earrings   15
    Points Necklace   18
    3 Squared Looped Earrings   22
    3 Squared Looped Necklace   26
    Quill Fan Earrings   31
    Quill Fan Necklace   33
    Double Triangle Earrings   36
    Double Triangle Necklace   40
Cylinder Designs
    Small Bugle Bead Earrings   45
    Bugle & Seed Bead Earrings   49
    Cylinder Combination Earrings   54
Peyote Designs   59
    Peyote Circle Earrings   60
    Small Circle with Large Bugle Earrings   62
    Small Circle with Quills Earrings   65
    Peyote Heart Earrings   67
Deco Designs
    Fan & Rectangle Earrings   69
    Triangle Reverse Earrings   73
Pine Needle Designs   77
    Pine Needle Heart Earrings   81
        Optional Dangles   84
    Pine Needle Circle Earrings   87
    Pine Needle Tear Drop Earrings   91
Color Plates I through IV   Center of Book

ACKNOWLEDGMENTS

Special Thanks to:

Jeannie McFarland and Deon DeLange for the inspiration I have received from their work;

To my husband Michael and son Sean for their loving support;

and, to R. L. (Smitty) Smith for his illustrations, to Brenda Martin, Kris Sweat and Winona Whitney for proofing and suggestions.

ABOUT THE AUTHOR

Laura Reid has been a professional crafts woman and designer for over twelve years. She first learned bead work from an ancient Indian woman she met in South Dakota twenty-two years ago.

Since that time, she has increased her knowledge and experience in bead work, leather crafts, quill work and has mastered other old-time craft skills. These mediums continue to inspire her to design and create new and innovative items.

Presently, she lives in Northern Idaho where she is currently designing more jewelry and crafts; working with beads, quills, pine needles and raffia, semi-precious stones, crystals and gems. She is the author of *New Adventures in Beading Earrings*.

INTRODUCTION

For either the new or experienced crafts person, the bead work designs in this book are unique and original. The earring and necklace designs are meant to stimulate the creativity in the reader with the purpose of making something special, beautiful and uniquely different, as well as being fashionable. These projects can be profitable or they can be personal treasures or special gifts. In any case, they are easy to make and fun to create.

Each section includes a different technique that is explained in easy-to-understand terms and helpful diagrams that are also easy to follow. Each project is designed to stand alone but, in order to avoid a lot of repetition, they sometimes refer to projects explained earlier in the book. For a thorough understanding, the crafts person may want to at least read the early projects before starting. It is also strongly suggested that the *Introduction* be read as it contains a great deal of information.

The reader is encouraged to change colors to suit personal taste and, by using different kinds of beads, create other versions of the designs themselves. The possibilities can be endless and exciting. For other beautiful earring designs, see *New Adventures in Beading Earrings* also available from Eagle's View Publishing.

< < < > > >

Creating beautiful earrings is very rewarding. To make certain they are the best they can be, each project is detailed in instructions and graphic diagrams are included as a further guide. Also, after completion of each project are directions for the finishing touches. This will insure a more perfect product. So, to begin, there are several things to keep in mind that will make the bead work more successful:

(1) Because these designs are concerned with shape and form, it is extremely important that the beads used be uniform in size. Be careful in selecting both the bugle and seed beads. Bugle beads should be examined for broken ends and different lengths or widths; seed beads should be selected that are fairly even in size. This will insure evenness in the designs. In most packages or hanks there will be some irregular size beads and these should always be discarded.

(2) Size 3/0 bugle beads may be used with Size 11/° or Size 12/° seed beads. Size 2/0 bugle beads may be used with Size 12/° seed beads. Remember, concerning seed beads, the larger the number, the smaller the bead. For many of the designs, larger than normal bugle beads will be used and Size 10/° seed beads will do nicely with those.

(3) To store and organize beads, try using microwave "TV dinner" trays.

They are made of plastic, have 3 or 4 compartments and are very shallow. Beads in hanks or packages may be stored in the large portion, and loose beads can be placed in the smaller compartments. The loose beads are easily picked up with the beading needle because the trays are so shallow; these trays also stack nicely. Saucers or other shallow trays can be used.

(4) When purchasing beads make certain there are enough to finish the project. Often the dye lots of beads will be different and hard to match up.

(5) The thread used in all of the projects is NYMO (nylon) beading thread. Size A is used for the smaller bugle and seed beads, or where many passes need to be made between beads. Size AA may also be used. Size O is used for the larger beads or where only a few passes are necessary.

The length of thread should always be at least 2 1/2 yards long before beginning the work unless otherwise noted. The tail end thread (the end of the thread that is not pulled through the work) should measure at least 6" to 8" long, so that there will be plenty of room to put a needle on it and work back through the bead work. Keep the tail end thread taut, as well as the beading thread, as this will aid in handling the work and in maintaining the design as it forms. It is also a good idea to reinforce each step as it is completed by running the needle through the beads again in order to keep the design in shape.

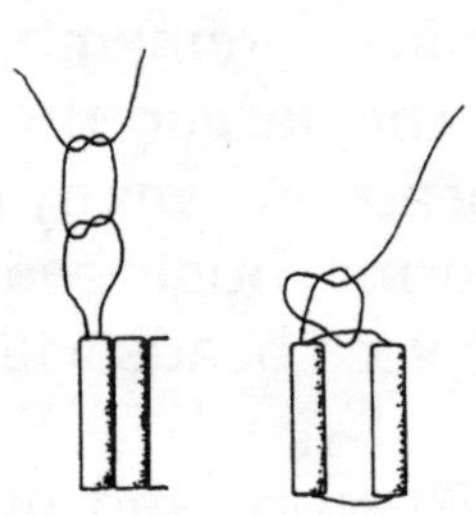

A single thread is used in all projects and, as it is nylon, there is some stretch to it and can be pulled up tightly and knotted securely.

Knotting the thread is made by using a simple overhand knot between the tail end thread and the needle thread, or by looping the needle thread between two beads, passing the needle through the center of the loop and pulling it tightly as shown in Figure 1 (the loop method). The thread that is between two attached beads is referred to as a **Junction**.

Adding a new thread is done by simply using the loop method with the needle thread at a **Junction Point** near the bead work in progress. In all cases, make the knots small and neat so that they do not detract from the beauty of the earring.

(6) The size of the beading needles used are either a Size 15/° English Beading Needle or a Size 10/° Japanese Beading Long Needle. The ones from England seem to be stronger; the ones from Japan or Taiwan have more flexibility.

(7) One thing to remember while the work is in progress is to move the beading needle up the thread often to avoid fraying the thread in the middle of the work.

(8) The work area should be one that has a flat surface covered with cloth or felt, with plenty of room for bead trays and tools. It is also important that it be a well lighted area. A table lamp or clamp-on elbow style lamp would be an asset while doing this close work to avoid eye strain.

(9) Because these earrings are shapes, a few extra steps need to be taken to make certain they maintain their form. By using super glue on the joints and applying clear fingernail polish over specified places, a more perfect product can be achieved. Read the glue instructions care-

Figure 1

fully, being mindful to keep fingers away from the area being glued.

In order to keep repetition to a minimum, only the first few projects in Part One include a description of how and where to apply super glue and/or clear fingernail polish to the joints. So, if choosing to start with a more complex project, be sure to be familiar with these instructions.

In all cases, the shapes can be manipulated until they conform and then the setting materials may be applied. This should be done on a flat surface and on material that will not be damaged by a spot of the polish or the glue.

(10) For small earrings or earrings that have few beads, the ear wires that may be hooked closed do very nicely. The french hook ear wires look best when placed on larger style earrings or those that have a lot of beads.

< < < > > >

Porcupine quills are used in a few of the designs, and can also be used in place of large bugles if desired. They can be purchased from Indian craft supply stores.

Sort out the quills that are long and uniform in size. Cut off the tips and ends. Clean them by simply using warm soapy water and a cloth or paper towel and wipe them free of dirt and oil.

It is possible to ascertain how much of the brown tip to cut off the quill by first cutting off the very tip, putting a seed bead up to it and seeing how much of it goes inside the bead. If too much off the tip is removed, when threaded on against a seed bead and pulled up tight it will go over the seed bead and cause the work to look irregular. If too little is cut off, it will go inside the seed bead. It should fit next to a seed bead the way a bugle bead would,

using the proper size of both.

To use the quills, measure each one for the project intended and cut them to size by cutting the white bottom portion only, as the tips should have already been clipped or cut. When working with quills, use a thimble and needle-nose pliers with which to pull the needle through the quills; or, it is possible to pass a larger needle through the white pitch inside the quill thereby making a larger space inside the quill for the needle to pass. In either case, go directly through the middle of the quill and not along the inside edge.

Store the rest of the quills in cans, boxes or heavy plastic bags. The quills may be sorted into many different sizes for different projects and kept separate by putting them in envelopes with the size written on the outside.

The reader may want to consult Jean Heinbuch's book *A Quillwork Companion* for a detailed account of the traditional and contemporary uses of porcupine quills.

< < < > > >

In the Pine Needle Earrings, the needles must be very long to be useful. In the South, needles from the Long Leaf or Loblolly Pine will work; in the West, those from the Ponderosa, Digger or Coulter Pines are suitable. The best needles will vary in length from 6" to 8" or longer. One group of pine needles has three separate needles to it, held together by a pitchy bud. Scalding water should be poured over the needles in a pan and allowed to soak for an hour. Then they should be wrapped in a damp towel for three more hours until the needles are pliable. When flexible, they can be left in the towel while the work progresses. Before beginning the work, the bud should be clipped off.

The Raffia is used to decorate and hold the work together and it can be purchased from any craft supply store. The long grasses should be unbundled and a long grass selected for the work. It is then split down the center and pulled apart to get different widths; from one grass you may get two to four strands. Use a crewel needle (blunt tip needle) to work with the raffia and pine needles.

The use of wire shapes wrapped in raffia and pine needle work has been used exclusively in basket making for many years. Many new craft ideas have been generated from this lovely technique. Therefore, the idea of using this portion of a basket making technique for earrings does not originate from the author, yet the bead work used to fill the shapes are of her own design and bead work technique.

For more design ideas, there are a number of good books on basketry, and on the use of pine needles and raffia. It is suggested that these sources be consulted to stimulate creativity in new earrings. Of special interest are two books written by Jeannie McFarland: *Pine Needle Raffia Basketry* and *Advanced Pattern Book for Pine Needle Raffia Basketry*. These books are not directed toward making earrings, but the basic stitches are very similar and may lead the reader to other techniques. It is possible to obtain these books and metal forms, similar to those used in this book, from McFarland's Floatel, P.O. Box 159, Thorne Bay, AK 99919.

<<<>>>

To make this book work and allow the use of creative expression, the following information may be helpful:

There will be some designs that are preferred to others. Select one project after reading the index or thumbing through the book until finding one that is desired. Gather the materials required. Then take a look at the legend and see if the color combinations are wanted. Carefully read through the directions a few times before actually begining. By studying the pictures and illustrations it is possible to visualize the process. When ready to begin, read each step through. Do the work and leave it momentarily to read the next step thoroughly, then continue. This way more confidence will be felt to begin and complete the project.

Complementary colors are as important in creating a beautiful set of earrings as in choosing the style preferred. To get a different idea of color combinations, check out the appropriate wardrobe. Perhaps there is a tendancy to focus on one color more than others. Some people also tend to look better with silver jewelry and others in gold, so place silver or gold colored beads next to a favorite color and choose a complementary color that looks good with these. When the project is completed, it will be a piece of jewelry with the proper color combination that is a beautiful matching accessory to the particular wardrobe selection made.

If a project is selected that is to be changed, study the information on Foundations, Ear wire Loops and Dangles. Make a drawing of the project with the changes selected and a special note of appropriate changes or adjustments in the instructions. This part of creating unique designs can be exciting.

If the purpose is to create earrings to sell as a product, be mindful that each new season has its own particular color combination in fashion. By studying the newest fashion magazines or by going to clothing stores, one will notice those outstanding colors and will get ideas from there.

I hope these new innovative designs are fun to make and as rewarding to the reader as they are to the author. ENJOY.

THE BASICS

This section will call specific attention to the variations shown in this book for Foundations, Ear wire Loops and Dangles. By combining different variations with the earrings shown, new designs can be created.

FOUNDATIONS

The foundation is a row of beads to which other beads are attached. The foundation can be very simple or can be a variation from many beading techniques.

The FIRST STYLE of foundation is used in the first project section (Points) and is done by simply threading on a desired number of bugle and/or seed beads, then threading back through them to form a loop or circle as shown on Page 18.

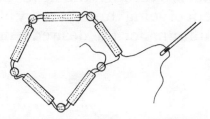

Figure 2

The SECOND STYLE of foundation is the bugle foundation and is shown on Page 15. It is made by threading on two bugle beads. A needle passes up through the first bead and down the second. A third bugle is threaded on, and the needle passes down through the second bugle and then up through the third. Another bugle is threaded

on and the needle passes up the third and down the fourth. This process is continued until the desired number of beads are completed. Any number of bugle beads may be used in this foundation and it is important to go back through the work to strengthen it; in all of the designs, the thread will go back through the work. This is very important in holding the work secure (Figure 3).

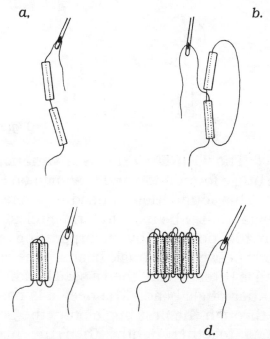

a.   b.

c.   d.

Figure 3

The addition of seed beads to the bugle bead foundation is done by threading on one seed bead and passing the needle under the thread between bugles 1 and 2 from the back to the front. To secure this bead, the needle will go back up through the seed bead only. Then another seed bead is threaded on and the process is repeated (Figure 4a). In some of the projects, this same technique is used to add bugle beads, as shown in Figure 4b.

9

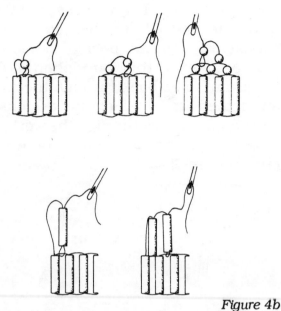

The FOURTH STYLE of foundation is made by using a straw, or a toothpick, as a form, using sets of bugle bead foundations and threading them together to create one piece to which other beads are attached.

Figure 6

Figure 4b

The THIRD STYLE is a variation of the bugle foundation and is shown on Page 31. This foundation is used to make the fans (and may be used to form circles) and is made possible by incorporating seed beads between the bugle beads. One bugle bead is threaded on, then a seed bead, then another bugle bead. The needle is passed up through the first bugle only, the beads pulled together tightly, then the needle passes through the seed bead and then down the second bugle bead. Another bugle bead is threaded on, then a seed bead. The needle passes down the second bugle and then up the third bugle, bypassing the second seed bead. Going back in reverse is done to strengthen the foundation (Figure 5).

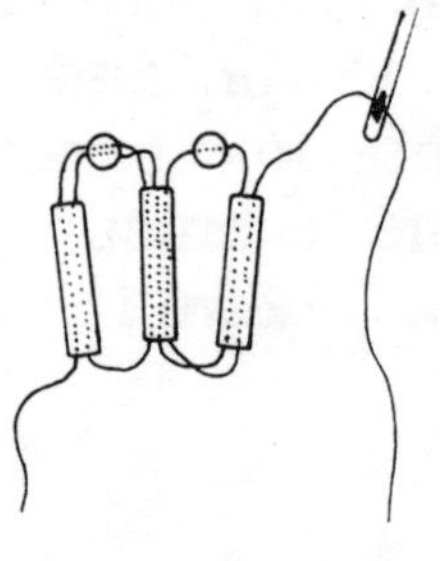

The FIFTH STYLE, shown on Page 59, is made with the peyote stitch. Almost any desired length may be made with the foundation. A certain number of beads are threaded on, and then gone back through to form a loop. A new bead is threaded on, going past one foundation bead and the needle passes through the next. So, it is a movement of going through every other one and continuing for the desired length.

Figure 7

The beads used for placement of ear wire loops and dangles on the peyote stitch are referred to as Anchor Beads. This is a technique where the thread will go through one side of a certain bead and come out the other and through selected beads, then

Figure 5

back again. This may be seen on Page 61.

Figure 8

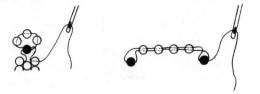

The SIXTH STYLE of foundation is the use of wire and raffia. The desired length of wire is cut to twice the amount needed for the shape chosen, as half of the entire length will be used for twisting the ends together. Then with the raffia, begin on the inside of the shape chosen and begin wrapping the wire using a blanket stitch. When the inside is complete, thread through the blanket stitch and begin doing the outside of the wire with the same stitch (see Page 77).

EARWIRE LOOPS

There are five styles of making the ear wire loops for the earring designs in this book and, while shown for specific earrings, are shown here:

STYLE #1 - Come up through the appropriate seed bead, thread on the required number of beads, pass the thread through them again, and down the other side of the work, pulling the beads together tightly.

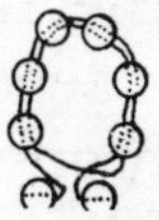

Figure 9

STYLE #2 - This style requires a certain number of beads threaded to sit on top of a lengthwise bugle bead Figure 10).

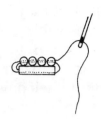

Figure 10

The needle then passes through these seed beads until the middle two are reached. The needle comes out, and the required number of seed beads are threaded on, gone through again to form a loop and then gone back through the center two seed beads, through the loop again, then out through the remaining seed beads that lie on top of the bugle (Figure 11).

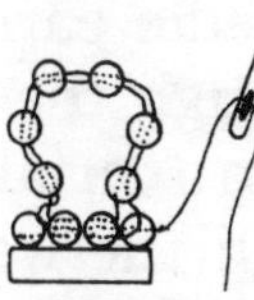

Figure 11

STYLE #3 - This style requires the use of anchor beads and is used with cylinder-style and peyote stitch earrings. A seed bead on one side, with another in line with it, is used by threading through it, threading on the number of seed beads required and then passing the needle over to the seed bead on the other side where the needle will go through it, then up and through the seed beads that form the loop. The needle then goes over and through the other side of the anchor bead and is knotted at a junction.

Figure 12

STYLE #4 - This is used on the pine needle earrings but may be added to other styles where desirable. A bugle bead is threaded on, then 6 to 8 beads, going through them again to form a loop, and the needle is brought back down the bugle and through the rest of the work. The thread is then knotted and clipped off.

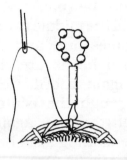

Figure 13

STYLE #5 - This ear wire loop is used for the pine needle earring only. Passing the needle through the pine needle at the top, threading on a certain number of beads, passing through the work from the other side, coming out at the first bead, and threading the needle back through for strength. Continue by coming out where the beads began and going through the first half of them. Then thread on another group of seed beads, passing the needle underneath the loop and up through this new set of beads again, thus forming a second loop. Finish by making a knot and going back through the work until the excess thread can be clipped off.

Figure 14a

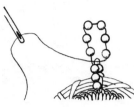

Figure 14b

DANGLES

There are several new earring designs that include adding seed beads, bugle beads and/or quills for dangles. As there are many different styles of dangles, a whole new earring look may be created just by substituting one style for another.

STYLE #1 is made by threading on a single line, or strand, of seed and/or bugle beads, adding 3 seed beads to the bottom, and then taking the needle back through the beaded strand while skipping the last 3 seed beads.

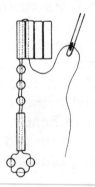

Figure 15

Then pass the needle through the foundation bugle or seed beads. By pulling the thread up with one hand and pulling the center bead of the last three with the other hand, the dangle will be tightened and straightened out. One thing to keep in mind is that the dangles should not be pulled up too tightly as they will be stiff and have no freedom to swing. Also, do not allow the dangles to hang too loosely as this would allow the thread to show. Shown below are four possible variations.

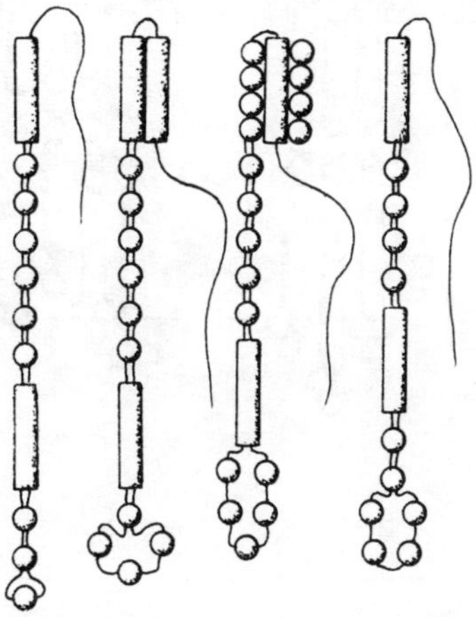

Figure 16

STYLE #2 is called a multi-loop. This is done by going down the first bugle, threading on the required number of beads, and working across to the end bugle and up through it. Then work the needle back through the foundation to the first bugle, go down it, thread on the number of beads required (there will be more than the first loop to create a draping effect) then going back up through the end bugle.

Figure 17

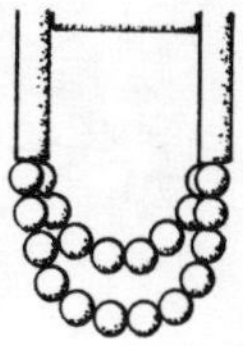

To this second style, a third strand may be added with six or more beads for a variation.

Figure 18

STYLE #3 is a straight loop dangle. Thread on the desired number of beads and then take the needle up through a bugle and the first few beads only.

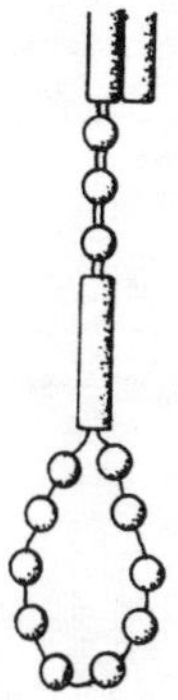

Figure 19

This loop dangle can be lengthened or shortened depending upon the look preferred. The number of beads may be increased or decreased on the thread, as shown below.

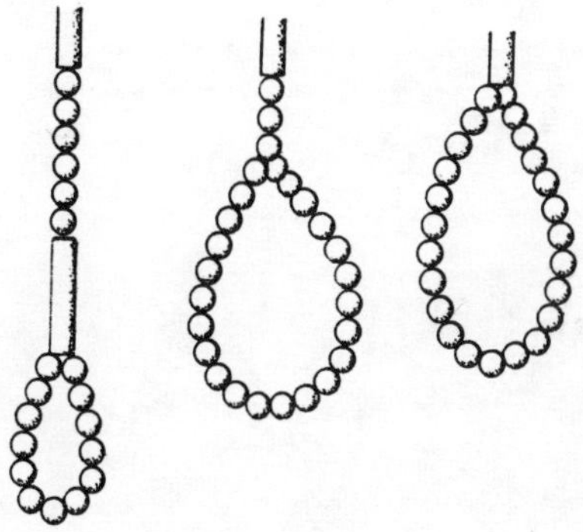

Figure 20

Other variations of these three styles may used. On the next page are a few illustrations using Style #1: By adding a few more beads to each strand until reaching the center and then decreasing equally to the other side, it creates a "V" effect. By decreasing a few beads on each strand the center is reached and then increasing by the same number, it will make an inverted "V" form (Figure 21).

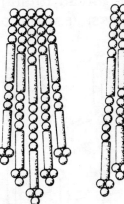

Figure 21

NOTES

FOUNDATION DESIGNS

DOUBLE POINT EARRINGS

Materials Required

Size O or A Nymo Thread
Size 15 Beading Needle
Size 3/0 Bugle Beads
Size 11/° Seed Beads
Clear Fingernail Polish

Step 1. Using a thread 2 yards long, thread on 2 bugle beads. Take the needle back up the first bugle bead and then down the second bugle bead. Thread on a third bugle bead. Take the needle down the second bugle bead, up the third bugle bead and then thread on a fourth bugle bead in the same manner (Figure 1). Then go back through the work for additional strength.

Figure 1

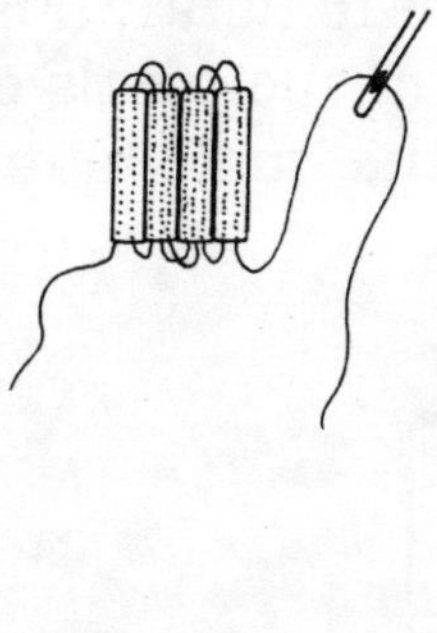

Step 2. As shown in Figure 2, with the needle coming out of the first bugle bead, thread on one seed bead and take the needle, from the back to the front, underneath the junction thread between the first and second bugle bead. Then take the needle up through the seed bead. Repeat this step twice more, so that there are three seed beads attached (Figure 3).

Figure 3

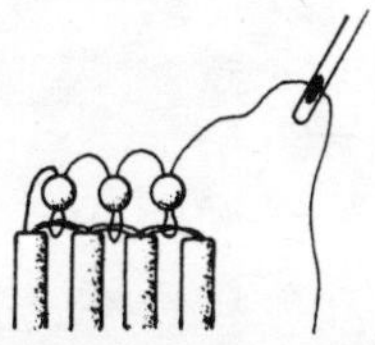

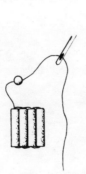

Step 3. This step involves making the ear wire loop and closing the bugle bead foundation at the same time. Turn the work so that the needle thread is on the left side. Make the beaded ear wire loop by threading on six seed beads. Take the needle down through the first attached seed bead and

Figure 2

15

then down through the first bugle bead (Figure 4). Take the needle up the fourth bugle bead, bringing the first and fourth bugle beads together; then, take the needle down through the first bugle bead.

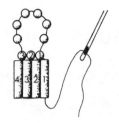

Figure 4

Step 4. The longest point for the earring will now be made. With the thread coming down and out of the first bugle bead, thread on five seed beads, one bugle bead, nine seed beads, one bugle bead, and six seed beads. Take the needle back through the fifth seed bead (of the six just threaded on) to make the tip (Figure 5).

Figure 5

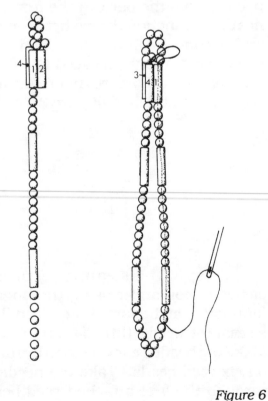

Figure 6

Thread on four seed beads, one bugle bead, nine seed beads, one bugle bead and five seed beads. Take the needle up through the fourth bugle bead of the foundation. Next, take the needle down the first bugle bead, then through all of the beads in the dangle (point) to the second seed bead on top of the second bugle bead (threaded on previously) and come out of this second seed bead, as shown in Figure 6.

Step 5. To make the flower in the point, thread on three seed beads, then take the needle through and out of the second seed bead on the other side (Figure

Figure 7

7). Thread on one seed bead. Take the needle through the second seed bead of the previous three seed beads, then thread on one seed bead, taking the needle down the first seed bead on top of the bugle bead, pulling the flower beads in tightly (Figure 8) and then back up all of the beads on this side and up through the bugle foundation bead.

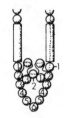

Figure 8

Step 6. Now take the needle down Number Two foundation bugle bead. Thread on eight seed beads, one bugle bead and six seed beads. As above, take the needle back through the five seed beads to make a tip. Thread on five seed beads, one bugle bead and eight seed beads. Take the needle up through Number Three foundation bugle bead, over and down through the foundation bugle bead Number Two (in front). Take the needle down the seed beads, bugle bead and through two seed beads, coming out of this second seed bead (Figure 9). Now, repeat Step 5 (above) for the flower insert. Work the needle up through a few beads and tie a looped knot. Go through more bead work and clip the thread off close to the work. Do the same for the tail end thread.

Figure 9

Finishing: Make the earring square at the top (bugle bead foundation) by squeezing in at the sides. Then apply clear fingernail polish to the front two bugle beads. Allow the work to dry completely.

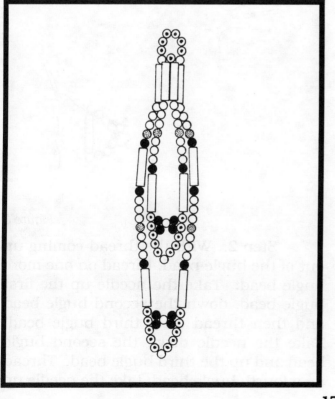

Legend

⬜ White 3/0 Bugle Bead

⊙ Transparent Orange Seed Bead

○ Yellow Seed Bead

● Medium Green Seed Bead

◉ Orange Seed Bead

POINTS NECKLACE

Materials Required

Size O or A Nymo Thread
Size 15 Beading Needle
Size 3/0 Bugle Beads
Size 11/° Seed Beads
Small Hook & Eye
or Barrel Necklace Clasp

Step 1. Using a thread 2 1/2 yards long, tie a knot through the ring of the necklace clasp. Repeat this several times, leaving a 5" tail end thread. Thread on nine seed beads. Take the needle through these beads again to form a circle. Repeat this technique once more for added strength. Then go through the first five seed beads (Figure 1). Thread on four seed beads, one bugle bead, four seed beads, then take the needle through the previous fifth seed bead (called the "crossing bead") as shown in Figure 2. As shown in Figure 3, take the needle through the four seed beads (on the right side) and up the bugle bead.

Figure 2

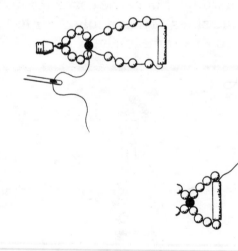

Figure 3

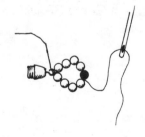

Figure 1

Step 2. With the thread coming up out of the bugle bead, thread on one more bugle bead. Take the needle up the first bugle bead, down the second bugle bead and then thread on a third bugle bead. Take the needle down the second bugle bead and up the third bugle bead. Thread on a fourth bugle bead, take the needle up through the third bugle bead, down and through the fourth bugle bead (Figure 4). Repeat this up and down movement once more between the third and fourth bugle beads to strengthen the work.

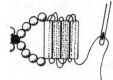

Figure 4

Figure 5

Step 3. As shown in Figure 5, thread on nine seed beads, take the needle down the fourth bugle bead, through the nine seed beads once more, down the fourth bugle bead and up through the five seed beads (right side). Now thread on four seed beads, one bugle bead and four more seed beads. Take the needle through the crossing bead (explained above), through the seed beads and the bugle bead again to strengthen the work, then through the four seed beads and down the bugle bead (Figure 6).

Now repeat Steps 2 and 3 (Figure 7) until the necklace measures 16" (Small), 18" (Medium) or 20" (Large), or the desired

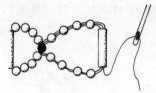

Figure 6

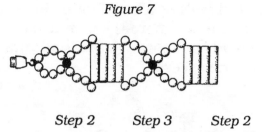

Figure 7

Step 2   Step 3   Step 2

length. If additional thread is needed, tie a knot at the junction thread between bugle beads and work the old thread back through the beadwork and clip off the excess. Attach a new thread at the junction thread between the bugle beads and continue working for an inch. Then, bring the tail end thread forward through the beadwork and clip off any excess close to the beadwork.

Figure 8

Step 4. When the desired length is complete make sure to end with a four bugle bead piece as created in Step 2; there should be an odd number of bugle bead sections and an even number of beaded X's. Then, as shown in Figure 8, thread on nine seed beads. Take the needle back through the last bugle bead, through the nine seed beads, through the last bugle bead again and then through five of the nine seed beads. Thread on eight seed beads. Take the needle through the crossing bead and then through the eight seed beads again. Repeat this step to strengthen these last eight seed beads. Take the needle through four seed beads, then through the ring of the necklace clasp, making a loop, coming up through the middle of the last beaded circle and making a knot (Figure 9). Repeat this knot a few more times and then take the thread back through the beadwork and clip off the excess.

Figure 9

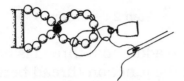

Step 5. In the following, the points (or dangles) will be added to the basic necklace created above. There are seven points to be placed and these will be located in the center front of the necklace. Find the middle set of foundation bugle beads and then count three sets to the left. Place the first point on this foundation by attaching a new 2 yard long thread by using the junction thread between the first and second bugle beads with a looped knot. Then take the needle up the second bugle bead (Figure 10).

Figure 10

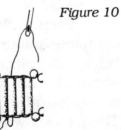

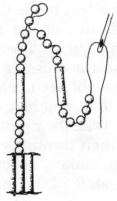

Figure 11

Step 6. Thread on five seed beads, one bugle bead and six seed beads. Take the needle back through the fifth seed bead, creating a tip, thread on four seed beads, one bugle bead and five seed beads (Figure 11). Take the needle down through the third bugle bead. Pull the thread taut and tie a knot between the junction thread. Then, take the needle up through the second bugle bead, up the five seed beads (on the left side of the point), up the bugle bead, up and out of the second seed bead, as shown in Figure 12. Thread on three seed beads. Take the needle down and out of the second seed bead on the right side of the

Figure 12

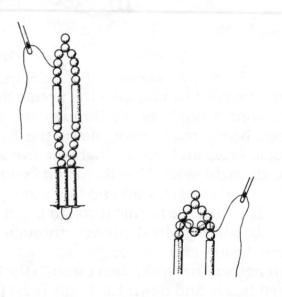

Figure 13

point (Figure 13). Thread on one seed bead. Take the needle through the second seed bead of the previous three (Figure 14). Thread on one seed bead, then take the needle down through the first seed bead on

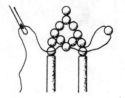

Figure 14

top of the left side bugle bead, through the bugle bead and the five seed beads below it (Figure 15). Pull the thread taut, squeezing the flower beads in place. Make a knot in the junction thread between the second and third bugle beads.

Figure 15

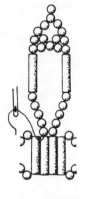

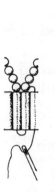

Figure 16

Step 7. Take the needle down through the second foundation bugle bead. Then take the needle up through the third bugle

Figure 17

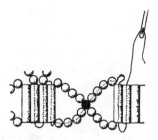

bead and down the fourth bugle bead (Figure 16). Take the needle through the seed beads of the cross, from the bottom left of the cross to the right top (Figure 17). Then take the needle down the first bugle bead and up the second bugle bead. Repeat Steps 6 and 7 until seven points are completed. Take the needle through the beadwork, tie a looped knot at a junction, go through a few more beads and clip off any excess thread close to the work. Repeat the same process for the tail end thread.

Legend

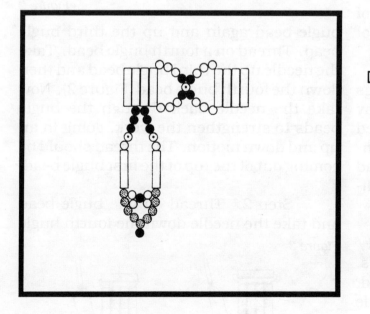

▭	White 3/0 Bugle Bead
⊙	Transparent Orange Seed Bead
○	Yellow Seed Bead
●	Medium Green Seed Bead
◉	Orange Seed Bead

3 SQUARED LOOPED EARRINGS

Materials Required

Size O or A Nymo Thread
Size 15 Beading Needle
Size 3/0 Bugle Beads
Size 10/° Seed Beads
Clear Fingernail Polish

For these earrings it is suggested that transparent silver-lined seed beads of all colors be used. A teaspoon of each of the following works well: silver, gold, light pink, rose, light green, dark green, yellow, light blue, dark blue, lavender, light orange and red. If the mix looks too "colored," add another teaspoon full of silver. Place all of the colors in a plate or on a large square of felt on a flat surface and mix them well.

The nice thing about these earrings is that any color bugle bead foundation may be used and the color will affect the seed beads, reflecting more of the complimentary color. Use a silver or gold bugle bead foundation and these earrings will coordinate easily with any outfit.

Step 1. With a thread measuring 1 1/2 yards long, thread on two bugle beads. Take the needle up the first bugle bead, bringing both bugle beads side by side (Figure 1). Take the needle down the second bugle bead and thread on a third bugle bead. Take the needle down the second

Figure 1

Figure 2

bugle bead again and up the third bugle bead. Thread on a fourth bugle bead. Take the needle up the third bugle bead and then down the fourth bugle bead (Figure 2). Now take the needle back through the bugle beads to strengthen the work, going in an up and down motion. The thread should be coming out of the top of the first bugle bead.

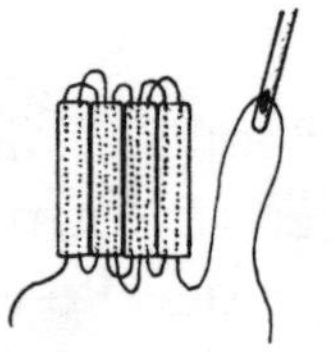

Step 2. Thread on one bugle bead and take the needle down the fourth bugle

Figure 3

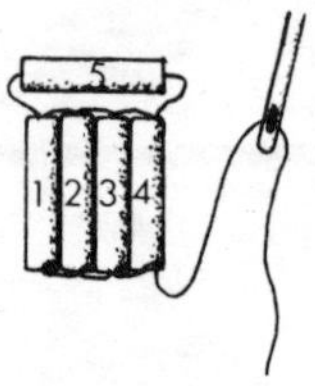

Figure 4

bead (Figure 3). Turn the work so that the bugle bead just threaded on is on the bottom of the bugle bead foundation. Thread on another bugle bead and take the needle down the end bugle bead (Figure 4). Pull the thread taut.

Step 3. Take the needle through the fifth bugle bead. Thread on one bugle bead and then take the needle back down the fifth bugle bead and up the bugle bead just threaded on (Figure 5). Thread on one more

Figure 5

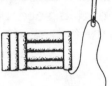

bugle bead. Take the needle up the previous bugle bead and then down the one just threaded on. Take the needle back up and down until the thread is coming out of the bottom of the first bugle bead (Figure 6). Take the needle through the bottom bugle bead (Number 4 of the four bugle bead foundation), then take the needle through the side bugle bead (Number 6) as illus-

Figure 6

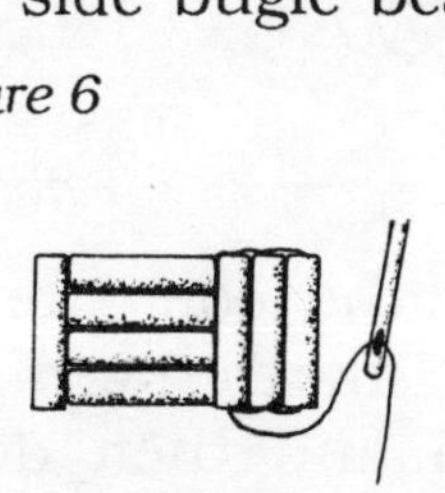

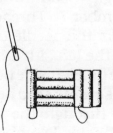

Figure 7

trated in Figure 7. Now turn the work so as to be working to the right (Figure 8). Thread on one bugle bead. Take the needle back down the first bugle bead and then up the second one. Thread on a third bugle bead. Then, take the needle up the second bugle bead and down the third one. Now, take the needle back through the bugle beads to strengthen the work. The needle should now be coming out of the bottom of the first bugle bead (Figure 9).

Figure 8

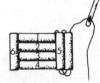

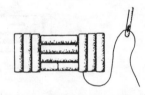

Figure 9

Step 4. This step will create the ear wire placement. Pass the needle through the bottom bugle bead of the center set (Number 1) and then turn the work so it once again becomes the top bugle bead. Then turn it over so that the thread is coming out of the left side (Figure 10). Thread on four seed beads, then take the needle back through this top bugle bead as

Figure 10

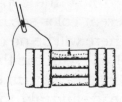

shown in Figure 11. Go through the four seed beads and the top bugle bead again for

Figure 11

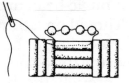

strength. Now take the needle through three seed beads. Thread on four seed beads and take the needle through the second and third foundation seed beads (Figure 12). Go through the four seed beads

Figure 12

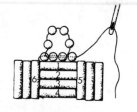

and the second, third and fourth foundation seed beads. Take the needle back through the top bugle bead and then down the first side bugle bead on the left side (Figure 13).

Figure 13

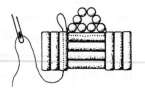

Step 5. To make the loops (or dangles), pick up a different color seed bead at random (so that there will be no color pattern, but a lot of color). With the thread coming down out of Bugle Bead Number 6, thread on forty seed beads and take the needle over and up through the first bugle bead on the right side (Number 5) and down through

Bugle Bead Number 7, as shown in Figure 14. Thread on fifty seed beads. Take the

Figure 14

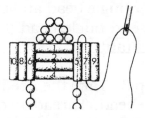

needle over and up through the second bugle bead on the left side (Number 8). Take the needle down the first bugle bead on the left side (Number 10) and thread on sixty-two seed beads. Take the needle up the third bugle bead on the right side (Number 9). Then take the needle down the second bugle bead (Number 7), up the first bugle bead (Number 5) and then through the top bugle bead of the center foundation (Number 1). Finally, go down the third bugle bead on the left side (Number 6). This is illustrated in Figure 15.

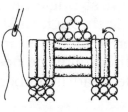

Figure 15

Step 6. To double the loops, thread on forty-five seed beads. Take the needle up Bugle Bead Number 5 and then down Number 7. Thread on fifty-five seed beads. Take the needle up the second bugle bead on the left side (Number 8) and then down the first left side bugle (Number 10). Thread on seventy seed beads, then take the needle up through the third bugle bead on the right side (Number 9) as illustrated in Figure 16. Make a looped knot at the junction between the bugle beads and then work through some of the bead work and clip off any excess thread close to the beads. Do the same for the tail end thread.

Finishing: Put clear fingernail polish on the bugle bead foundation only and allow the piece to dry completely.

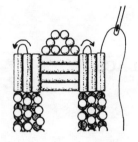

Figure 16

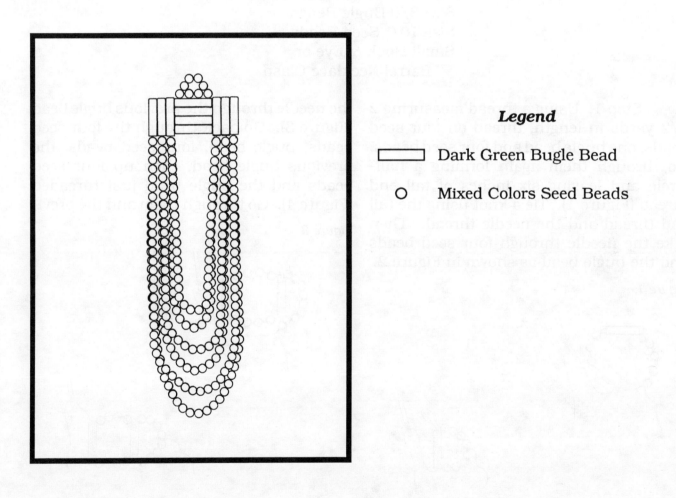

Legend

▭ Dark Green Bugle Bead

○ Mixed Colors Seed Beads

3 SQUARED LOOPED NECKLACE

Materials Required

Size 15 Beading Needle
Size O or A Nymo Thread
Size 3/0 Bugle Beads
Size 10/° Seed Beads
Small Hook & Eye or
Barrel Necklace Clasp

Step 1. Using a thread measuring 2 1/2 yards in length, thread on four seed beads, one bugle bead and four seed beads. Go through them again forming a half-circle and leaving six inches of tail end thread (Figure 1). Tie a knot using the tail end thread and the needle thread. Then take the needle through four seed beads and the bugle bead as shown in Figure 2.

Figure 1

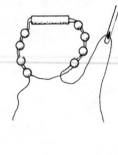

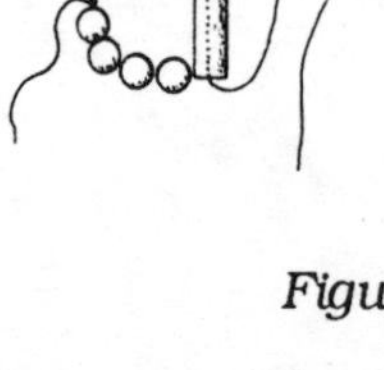

Figure 2

Step 2. Thread on four seed beads, one bugle bead and four seed beads. Take the needle through the previous bugle bead (Figure 3). Go back through the four seed beads, bugle bead, four seed beads, the previous bugle bead, then up four seed beads and the bugle bead just threaded (Figure 4). Go through them and the previ-

Figure 3

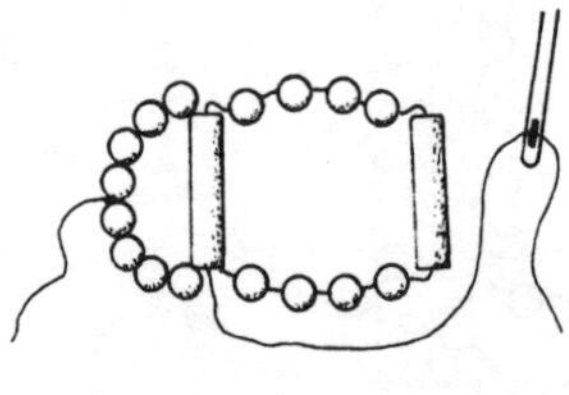

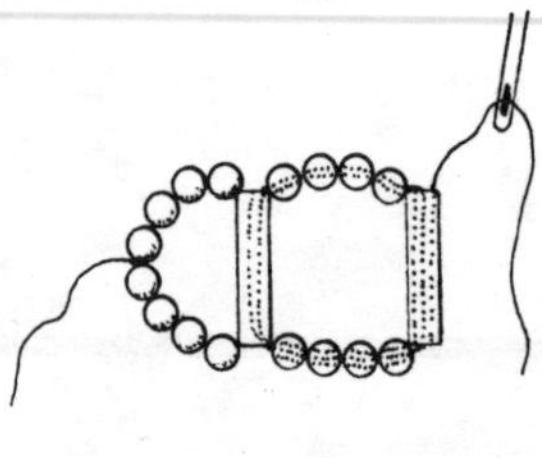

Figure 4

ous bugle bead again for added strength. Repeat Step 2 until the beaded work measures six inches (for a small size), seven

26

Figure 5

Figure 8

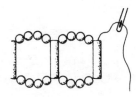

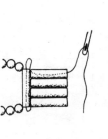

inches (medium) or eight inches (large size).

    Step 3. Turn the work so that the needle thread is coming out of the top of the bugle bead as shown in Figure 5. Thread on two bugle beads. Take the needle up the first bugle bead just threaded on and pull these two bugle beads close to the side bugle bead (Figure 6). Take the needle

Figure 6

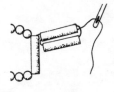

down through the second bugle bead and thread on another bugle bead. Continue as in making a four bugle bead foundation (shown in the Introduction and in prior projects). See Figure 7. Now take the

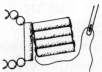

Figure 7

needle through the side bugle bead and up through the first bugle bead (of the four just made) as shown in Figure 8. Thread on one bugle bead. Take the needle through the bottom bugle bead of the four foundation beads, then up the left side bugle bead and

up through the first foundation bugle bead as shown in Figure 9. Take the needle down this new side bugle bead and thread on one bugle bead. Then take the needle down the first side bugle bead and up the second and continue to make a three bugle bead foundation (Figure 10).

Figure 9

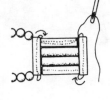

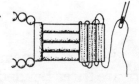

Figure 10

    Step 4. Turn the work over so that the needle is coming out of the top of the third bugle bead (Figure 11). Repeat Step 3 (above) until reaching Figure 9. Take the

Figure 11

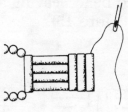

Figure 12

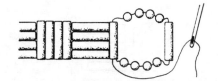

Figure 15

needle down this side bugle bead and thread on four seed beads, one bugle bead and four seed beads as shown in Figure 12. Take the needle down through the side bugle bead, then through the seed beads, bugle bead, seed beads, down through the side bugle bead, up through four seed beads and the new side bugle bead (Figure 13).

Step 6. With a new thread 2 1/2 yards long, attach the thread at the junction thread between the side bugle bead and the first bugle bead of the first four foundation bugle beads, making a looped knot (Figure 16). Take the needle through the first bugle bead (of the four bugle bead foundation), and down through the first

Figure 13

Looped Knot

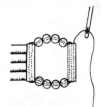

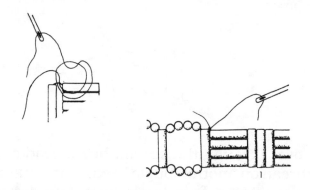

Figure 16

Step 5. Repeat Steps 3 and 4 until there are three beaded open ovals and eight four foundation side squares (Figure 14). Repeat Step 2 until this piece measures exactly the same (6", 7" or 8"). Thread on eight seed beads and take the needle back down the side bugle bead, through the eight seed beads, back through the side bugle bead again, then up through four seed beads. Tie a looped knot between the fourth and fifth seed bead, leaving a six inch tail end thread (Figure 15).

side bugle bead (of the three bugle bead foundation as shown in Figure 17). Thread on four inches of seed beads, then take the needle over to and up through the third bugle bead of the third set (of the three bugle bead foundations as shown in Figure 18). Take the needle down the second bugle

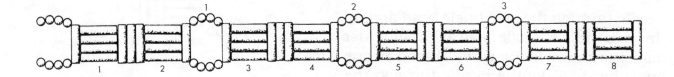

Figure 14

(next to the third bugle bead just used) and thread on three and a half inches of seed

Figure 17

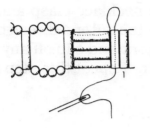

Figure 18

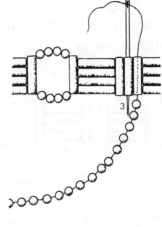

beads. Take the needle over and up through the second bugle bead (of the first bugle bead three foundation set as shown in Figure 19). Now, take the needle down the third bugle bead (next to the second bugle bead just used) and thread on two and a half inches of seed beads. Take the needle up the first bugle bead of the third bugle bead foundation set (Figure 20). Make a looped knot between the three bugle bead foundation and the four bugle bead foundation as shown in Figure 21. Work through some bead work and clip off close to the

work. Do the same thing for the tail end thread.

Step 7. Repeat Step 6, beginning

Figure 19

Figure 20

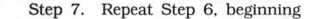

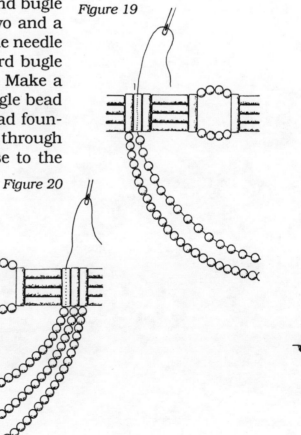

29

Figure 21

with the second three bugle bead foundation (Figure 22) and threading the seed beads to and through the fourth three bugle bead foundation set. Finish the threads in the usual manner.

Step 8. The tail end thread at each end of the necklace will now be used to attach necklace clasps (Figure 23). Put a needle on the tail end thread of one strand and work a knot several times between the ring of the necklace clasp and the beaded loop. Work the tail end thread back through the bead work and clip off any excess close to the work. Repeat this step for the other strand.

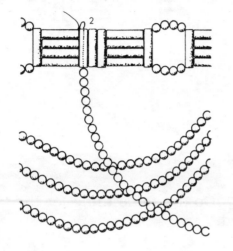

Figure 22

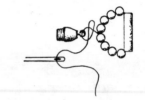

Figure 23

QUILL FAN EARRINGS

Materials Required

Size O or A Nymo Thread
Size 15 Beading Needle
Porcupine Quills -
    approximately 1" in length
Size 11/° Seed Beads
Small Disc Beads
Super Glue

Step 1. Using a thread measuring 1 1/2 yards long, thread on one quill (through the white end). Leave eight inches of tail end thread. Thread on six seed beads, one disc bead, six seed beads and one quill (from the dark end first) as shown in Figure 1. Tie the tail end thread and the needle thread together in a knot at the top of both quills, bringing them snugly together. As the tail end thread will be used to secure all of the quills, leave it uncut.

Step 2. Take the needle down through the first quill and the first seed bead. Thread on five seed beads, one disc bead, six seed beads and one quill (Figure 2). Tie the needle thread and the tail end thread together in a knot at the top. Take the needle down a quill and one seed bead. Repeat Step 2 once or twice more, depending upon how wide the fan is to be.

Step 3. Put a needle on the tail end

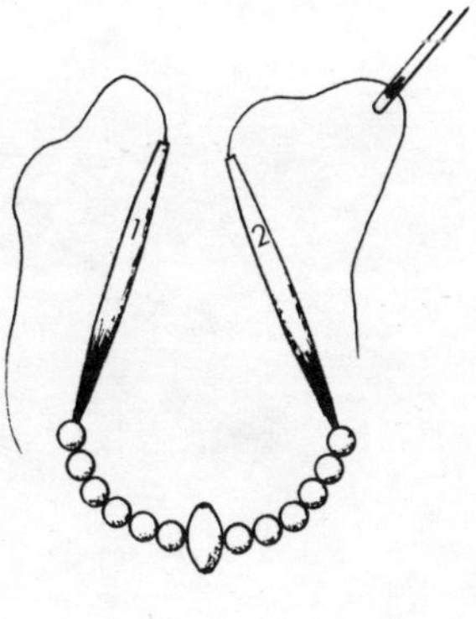

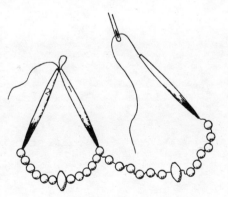

Figure 1

Figure 2

thread and work back through the quills and seed beads. Clip off any excess close to the work.

Step 4. With the needle thread, thread on six seed beads for the ear wire loop. Go through them again to form the loop close to the work, then take the needle down the end quill and one seed bead. Tie a knot and then go through the beadwork and clip off any excess thread.

Finishing: Straighten out the fan and apply super glue to the top of the quills and at the end of each quill. Allow to dry thoroughly.

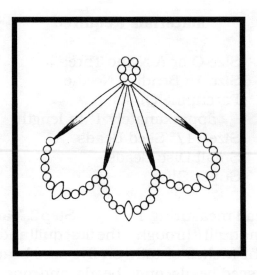

QUILL FAN NECKLACE

Materials Required

Size O or A Nymo Thread
Size 15 Beading Needle
Size 11/° Seed Beads
Porcupine Quills -
   approximately 1" in length
Small Disc Beads
Small Barrel Necklace Clasp
Super Glue

Step 1. Using a thread measuring 1 1/2 yards long, thread on one quill (through the white end). Leave eight inches of tail end thread. Thread on six seed beads, one disc bead, six seed beads and one quill (from the dark end). Tie the tail end thread and the needle thread together in a knot at the top of both quills bringing them snugly together (Figure 1). Leave the tail end thread uncut as it will be used to secure all of the quills.

Step 2. As shown in Figure 2, take the needle down through the first quill and the first seed bead. Thread on five seed beads, one disc bead, six seed beads and one quill. Tie the needle thread and the tail end thread together in a knot at the top. Take the needle down one of the quills and one seed bead, then repeat Step 2 once more.

Step 3. Put the needle on the tail end

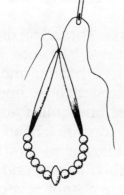

Figure 1

Figure 2

thread and work back through the quills and seed beads. Clip off any excess thread close to the beadwork.

Step 4. Replace the needle on the needle thread and thread on six seed beads. Go through them again to form the loop close to the tops of the quills, then take the needle down the end quill and one seed bead, tie a looped knot, go through more beadwork and clip off any excess thread.

Figure 3

Step 5. Using a new thread 1 1/2 yards long, tie a knot between the three seed beads of the loop and the top of the quill (Figure 3). Take the needle up the three seed beads (the third seed bead will be used as an anchor bead). Thread on one quill (from the dark end), three seed beads and one quill (from the light end first), as shown in Figure 4. Take the needle through

Figure 5

the anchor bead from the other side (Figure 5). Then up the first quill and through two of the seed beads; this second bead will now be used as an anchor bead. Thread on one seed bead, one quill, three seed beads, one quill and one seed bead. Take the needle back through the anchor bead from the other side, then up the first quill and through two of the top seed beads (Figure 6).

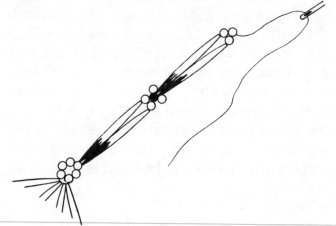

Figure 6

Step 6. Thread on one quill (from the dark end first), six seed beads, one disc bead, six seed beads, one quill (dark end first), six seed beads, one disc bead, six seed beads, one quill (dark end first), six seed beads, one disc bead, six seed beads, one quill (dark end first), and six seed beads. Attach to one end of the necklace clasp and tie a knot several times. Then, without cutting the thread, go back through

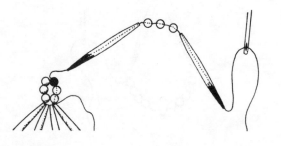

Figure 4

34

the entire strand to the second seed bead of the double quills. Pass the needle through the other side of this bead and back up the entire strand. Once again, go through the end of the necklace clasp and tie a knot. Then go back through some of the work and clip off the end of the thread close to the work.

Step 7. Repeat Steps 5 and 6 for the other side of the necklace strand.

Finishing: Work the tail end threads back through the work and clip off the excess thread close to the work. Apply super glue to the top and bottom ends of the quills on the various fans and allow to dry completely.

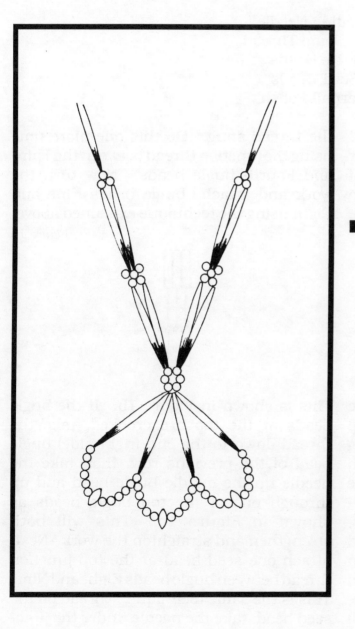

Legend

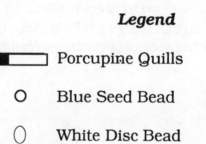 Porcupine Quills

O   Blue Seed Bead

◖   White Disc Bead

DOUBLE TRIANGLE EARRINGS

Materials Required

Size 15 Beading Needle
Size O or A Nymo Thread
Size 3/0 Bugle Beads
Size 10/° Seed Beads
Clear Fingernail Polish

Step 1. Using a thread measuring 2 yards in length, make a foundation of four bugle beads as shown in Step 1, Figure 1 of the Double Point Earrings on Page 15. Go back through the work for added strength.

Figure 1a

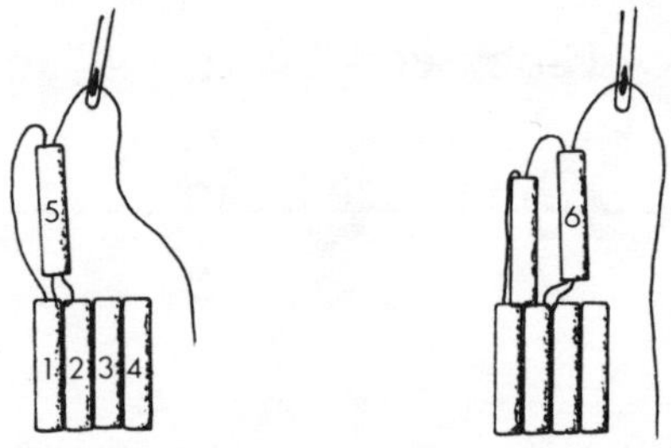

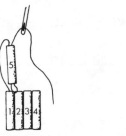

Now, as shown in Figure 1a, attach three bugle beads in the junction threads on top of the bugle beads. This is done by bringing the needle out of the far left bugle bead in the foundation, threading on one bugle bead, going under the junction thread between the First and Second bugle beads, going back through the added bugle bead and pulling the thread taut. Thread on another bugle bead, go under the thread between the Second and Third bugle beads, back through the new bugle bead and pull

the thread snug. Do this one more time using the junction thread between the Third and Fourth bugle beads. Now turn the work and attach bugle beads Nine and Eight using the technique explained above.

Figure 1b

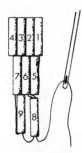

This is shown in Figure 1b. If the bugle beads at the top are crooked, take the thread down to the end (right side) bugle bead of the previous row, then take the needle up the middle bugle bead and up through one of the top bugle beads as shown in Figure 1c. This will both strengthen and straighten the work. Next, attach one seed bead at the top junction thread between bugle beads Eight and Nine: This is the same technique. Thread on the seed bead, take the needle under the junc-

With the thread coming out of the bottom right bugle bead, thread on three seed beads and two bugle beads. Take the needle back up the first bugle bead (see Figure 3) and down the second bugle bead. Turn the work and continue making a four bugle bead foundation (Figure 4).

Figure 4

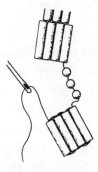

tion thread, back through the seed bead and pull the thread to hold in place. Then take the needle over and through the bugle beads on the right side (Figure 2).

Figure 2

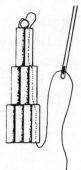

Now, as shown in Figure 5, repeat Step 1 from this point. With the thread coming out of the top seed bead of this second triangle, thread on six seed beads; these will be the beads for the ear wire. Take the needle over and down through the top seed bead of the first triangle (Figure 6).

Figure 5

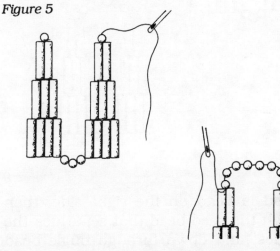

Figure 6

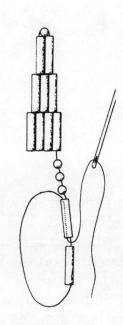

Figure 3

Step 3. Take the needle down through bugle bead Number Nine on the left side (see Figure 7). Thread on one seed bead, then take the needle up through Number

37

Figure 7

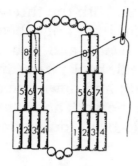

through the first bugle bead (right side), over and down through bugle bead Number Two as shown in Figure 10. Thread on twenty-five seed beads. Take the needle over and up through bugle bead Number

Figure 10

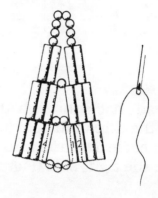

Eight on the right side. Take the needle up through the center seed bead, through the six seed beads for the ear wire, down the center seed bead on the left side, through bugle bead Number Nine and down through the Seventh bugle bead (Figure 8). Thread on two seed beads. Take the needle up the

Figure 8

Three on the left side. Then down through bugle bead Number Two (Figure 11) and thread on thirty-nine seed beads. Take the needle over to the right side and go up through bugle bead Number Three and

Figure 11

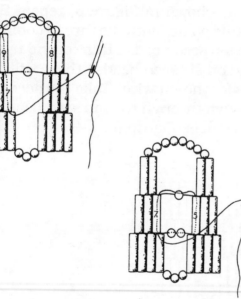

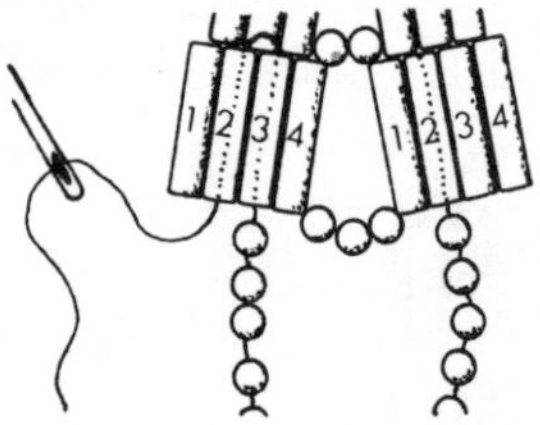

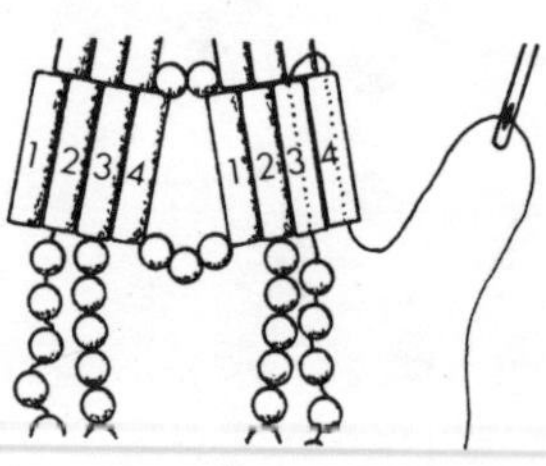

Figure 9

fifth bugle bead on the right side, then through the seed bead that separates the triangles, and down through bugle bead Number Seven on the left side (Figure 9).

Step 4. With the thread coming down out of bugle bead Number Seven, go down through the fourth bugle bead and the three seed beads. Take the needle up

Figure 12

down through Number Four (Figure 12). Thread on fifty-four seed beads and take the needle over and up through bugle bead Number One on the left side.

Step 5. This step will double the beaded loop dangles now in place. Take the needle down through bugle bead Number Two on the left side, thread on thirty-five

38

seed beads and then go over and up through Number Three on the right side and down through bugle bead Number Four. Coming down and out of Number Four on the right side, thread on fifty seed beads. Take the needle up through Number One on the left side, as shown in Figure 13. Now take the needle down the Second bugle bead, up the Third, down the Fourth, through the three seed beads, up bugle bead Number One (right side) and down through the Second bugle bead (Figure 14). Thread on seventeen seed beads. Take the needle over and up through the Third bugle bead on the left side.

Step 6. Take the needle up the left side, through Number Six and Eight. Tie a knot at the junction (Figure 15). Thread through the work and clip off any excess thread close to the work. Work the tail end thread in the same manner.

Figure 15

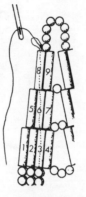

Finishing: Clear fingernail polish should be lightly applied to both bugle triangles only. Allow to dry thoroughly.

Figure 13

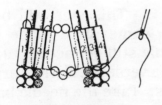

Figure 14

Legend

▬▬ Cobalt Blue Bugle Bead

▭ Crystal Bugle Bead

● Cobalt Blue Seed Bead

○ Crystal Seed Bead

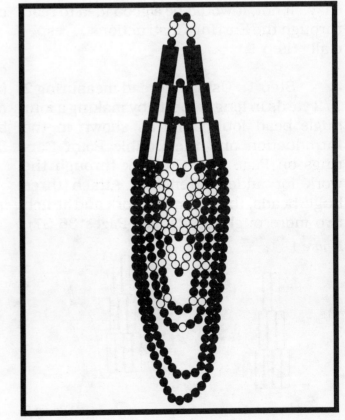

39

DOUBLE TRIANGLE NECKLACE

Materials Required

Size 15 Beading Needle
Size O or A Nymo Thread
Size 3/0 Bugle Beads
Size 10° Seed Beads
Small Hook & Eye or
Barrel Necklace Clasp

This project relies heavily on the techniques explained and illustrated in the Double Triangle Earrings (Pages 36 - 39). If that project has been made, this one will be easy. If not, it would be a good idea to read through the Earrings instructions . . . especially Step 1.

Step 1. Using a thread measuring 2 1/2 yards in length, begin by making a four bugle bead foundation as shown in the Introduction and the Double Point Earrings on Page 15. Go back through the work for added strength. Attach three bugle beads, then turn the work and attach two more bugle beads (see Pages 36-37).

Figure 1 shows the completed step. Take the needle down the right side bugle bead of the previous row and through the end bugle bead of the foundation (Figure 2). Thread on three seed beads.

Step 2. This step will be creating exactly the same piece made in Step 1 (above), while still connected to the previous piece. Reverse the work. Thread on two bugle beads. Take the needle back up the first bugle bead, pulling the work up close

Figure 1

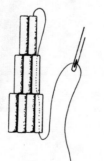

Figure 2

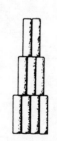

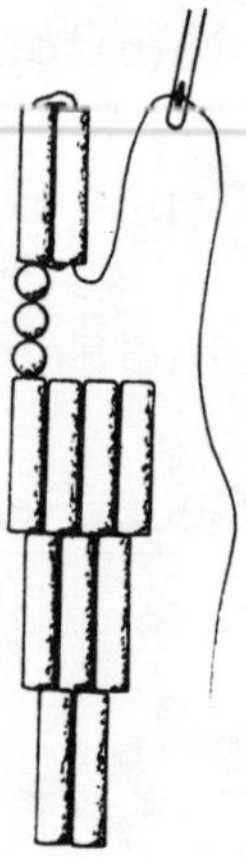

Figure 3

Figure 4

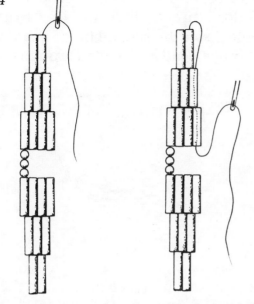

Figure 5

to the third seed bead, and then down the second bugle bead (Figure 3). Then continue this to make a four bugle bead foundation. Turn the work and, as in Step 1, attach three bugle beads, turn the work and attach two more bugle beads (Figure 4). Take the needle down to and through the end bugle bead of the previous row as

shown in Figure 5. Thread on three seed beads. Take the needle down the end bugle beads of the previous set (Figure 6). Tie a looped knot at a junction thread, work the thread through some of the beadwork and clip off any excess. One piece is now completed.

Step 3. Repeat Steps 1 and 2 until there are three complete pieces (or more if desired). Please note that one of these pieces may be made into a simple earring by adding six seed beads on the top two bugle beads and one seed bead to the other end. An additional option may be made by using longer bugle beads, or adding more seed beads between the sets, to create a very long dangling earring. Examples of these options can be seen in Figure 7.

Figure 7

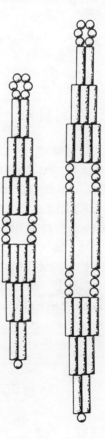

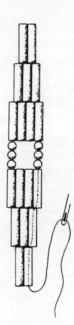

Figure 6

Step 4. Using a new thread 2 1/2 yards long, attach this thread to the necklace clasp ring using an overhand knot and repeat this knot several times for added strength. Leave a six to eight inch tail end thread. Thread on six inches (for a small necklace), eight inches (medium) or ten of the second end bugle bead using the junction thread (Figure 11). Bring the needle down the second bugle bead, up the first bugle bead and again through the seed bead. One piece is now attached.

Step 5. Thread on four seed beads.

Figure 8

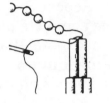

Figure 11

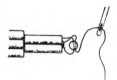

inches (large) of seed beads. Take the needle through from the back of the junction thread, between the end two bugle beads of one of the pieces made above (Figure 8). Now go through the last seed

Take the second piece and using the junction thread between the two bugle beads, attach the last seed bead added (Figure 12). Take the needle down the second bugle bead, up the first bugle bead, up the seed

Figure 9

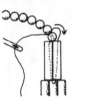

Figure 12

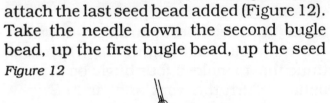

bead of the strand (Figure 9), then down the second bugle bead, back up the first bugle bead and up through the seed bead. Repeat this last movement again for added strength. Now take the needle through the end bugle beads, through the three seed beads, and then the end bugle beads as shown in Figure 10. Attach one seed bead to the top

bead, back down the second bugle bead and through the end bugle bead in each section (as shown in Figure 10). Attach one seed bead in the junction between the two end bugle beads as described above and then repeat Step 5 for the last piece.

Step 6. With the three pieces worked

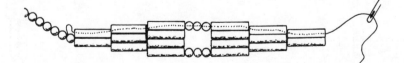

Figure 10

together, attach a seed bead on the top of the two end bugle beads in the last piece as explained above. Then thread on exactly the same number of seed beads that were threaded on the other side of the necklace (before the first piece). Attach the thread to the other ring of the necklace clasp using an overhand knot. Repeat the knot several times. Then go back through the strand and continue through the other (left) side and tie another knot. Work the end threads through the bead work and clip off any excess close to the work.

Figure 13

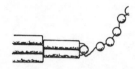

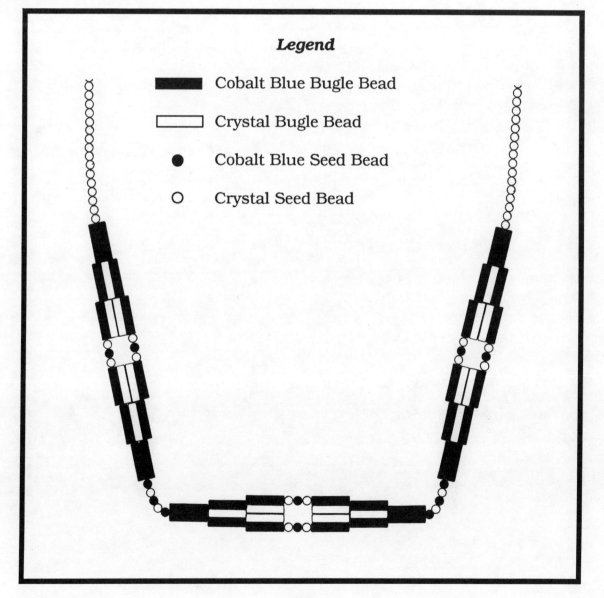

Legend

▬▬ Cobalt Blue Bugle Bead

▭ Crystal Bugle Bead

● Cobalt Blue Seed Bead

○ Crystal Seed Bead

NOTES

CYLINDER DESIGNS

SMALL BUGLE BEAD EARRINGS

Materials Required

Size O or A Nymo Thread
Size 15 Beading Needle
Size 2/0 Bugle Beads
Size 11/° Seed Beads
Cocktail Straw
Clear Fingernail Polish

Please Note: The circumference of drinking straws may vary but, in order to keep away from a great deal of repetition just to account for every difference in size, this project assumes that all cocktail straws are the same size. For example, it is assumed that it will require nine bugle beads to go around the straw. As you do this project, if you find that it takes only eight bugle beads or ten of them, be sure and make that adjustment throughout the work.

Step 1. Using a single thread that measures 1 1/2 yards in length, make a foundation row of nine bugle beads or of a length that will fit the circumference of the cocktail straw (see Introduction or Step 1 in Double Point Earrings, Page 15). To do this, as the foundation row is being made, periodically hold it around the straw until the correct length has been made; as noted above, it is assumed in the following directions that it will require nine bugle beads to go around the straw. Then, thread back through the bugle beads for added strength. Next attach seed beads across the top of the foundation by threading on one seed bead, taking the needle under the junction thread between the first and second bugle bead (from the back to the front) and then going up through the seed bead (Figure 1). Con-

Figure 1

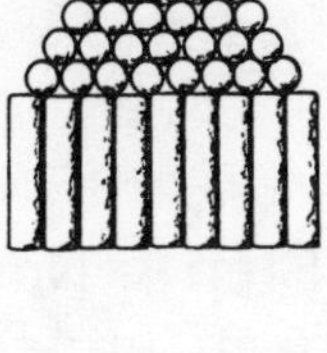

Figure 2

tinue this technique until there is a seed bead between each of the bugle beads. With nine bugle beads there should be eight seed beads in place. Turn the work over, so that the eighth seed bead is on the left side and attach seven seed beads in the same manner using the junction threads between the eight seed beads in the first row. Repeat attaching seed beads and turning the work until four rows of seed beads have been completed as shown in Figure 2. (The top row will have five seed beads.)

Figure 3

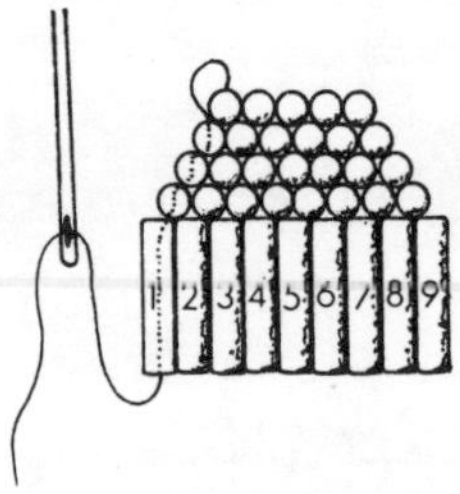

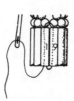

Step 2. The needle and thread should be at the left of the work. Take the needle down through the end seed bead of the third row, then through the end (left side) seed beads of rows two and one and finally down through the first bugle bead (Figure 3). Take the needle over and up through the ninth bugle bead, thus bringing the bugle bead ends together to form a small ring. As shown in Figure 4, pull the thread up tight and pass the needle over and down through the first bugle bead. Repeat the threading through for added strength.

Figure 4

Step 3. Now that the bugle bead ends have been joined together, this step will involve bringing the beaded end rows to-

gether. Take the needle back up the ninth bugle bead and then up through the first row end seed bead. The thread will be at the right side of the work. Now take the needle over and down through the end seed bead on the left side of the first row (Figure 5). Then, take the needle over and up through

Figure 5

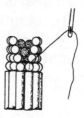

the right side end seed bead of the first row. Pull the thread up tightly as shown in Figure 6. Repeat this process for the second, third and fourth row end seed beads. When this is complete, the needle and thread should be at the right side.

Figure 6

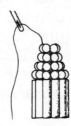

Step 4. Take the needle over to the left end seed bead (top row), go through it and then go up through the seed bead on the left next to this one (Figure 7). To make the ear wire loop, thread on six seed beads and pass the needle over (to the right side)

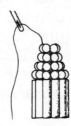

Figure 7

and down through the corresponding seed bead; this will be the seed bead next to the end seed bead. Now, take the needle up through the six seed beads just threaded on, over and down through the second seed bead on the left side where this started. Pass the needle over and up the end seed bead on the left side then tie a knot at the nearest junction. Take the thread through the end seed beads and clip off any excess thread close to the work. Work the tail end thread in the same way. Finally, slip this work over the straw and leave it at the top (see the top of Figure 8).

Figure 8

2 1/2 yards long, pass the needle up and through the bottom section of any bugle bead, leaving a six inch tail end thread. Continue passing the needle through a bugle bead of each section (thereby lining all sections up) but do not take the needle through the seed bead at the top. Take the needle over and down through the next bugle bead and all of the bugle beads beneath it . . . as if it were one long bugle bead. Tie the tail end thread and needle thread together in a knot at the bottom. Then, continue with the needle thread up and down through all sets until they are all attached and lined up. The thread should be at the bottom of the work (Figure 9). The work should be tight.

Figure 9

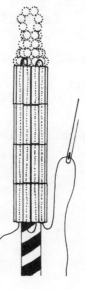

Step 5. As explained in Step 1, make three more separate foundations of nine bugle beads. This will be the foundation set only; without the added seed beads. Finish off the thread ends in the usual manner. Then, slip each set on the straw underneath the previous set as shown in Figure 8.

Step 6. With a new thread measuring

Step 7. Place a needle on the tail end thread and work it through to the top and clip off any excess close to the work. With the needle thread, while the entire piece remains on the straw, thread on the dangles following the diagram (the sequence being: six seed beads, one bugle bead, six seed beads, one bugle bead, six seed beads, one bugle bead, six seed beads, one bugle bead, six seed beads, one bugle bead, six seed

47

beads, one bugle bead, six seed beads, one bugle bead, six seed beads and then back through the first bugle bead and the top six seed beads). Pass the needle thread back up the cylinder line and over to the next line and down as if it were one long bugle bead. Then begin threading on the next strand of beads for the dangle. Repeat until all nine dangles are in place. Finally, make a knot at a junction and work through a few seed beads before removing any excess thread.

Option: Instead of the four sets of small bugle beads, use a long, one inch bugle bead. Make one foundation of the long bugle beads, do the same seed bead work, slip this over the straw and attach the dangles as explained above.

Finishing: Brush clear fingernail polish over the entire cylinder only and allow to dry overnight.

Legend

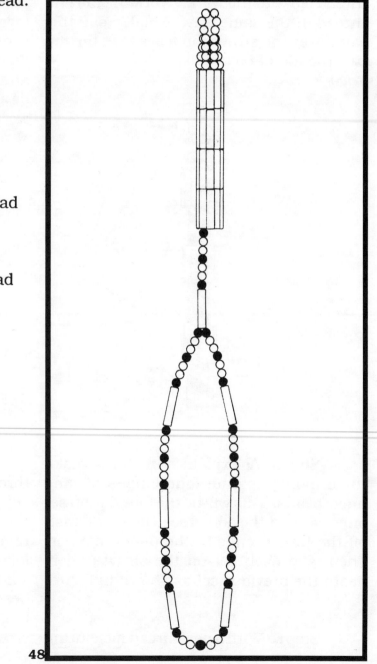

☐ Silver-Lined Purple Bugle Bead

● Black Bugle Bead

○ Transparent Purple Seed Bead

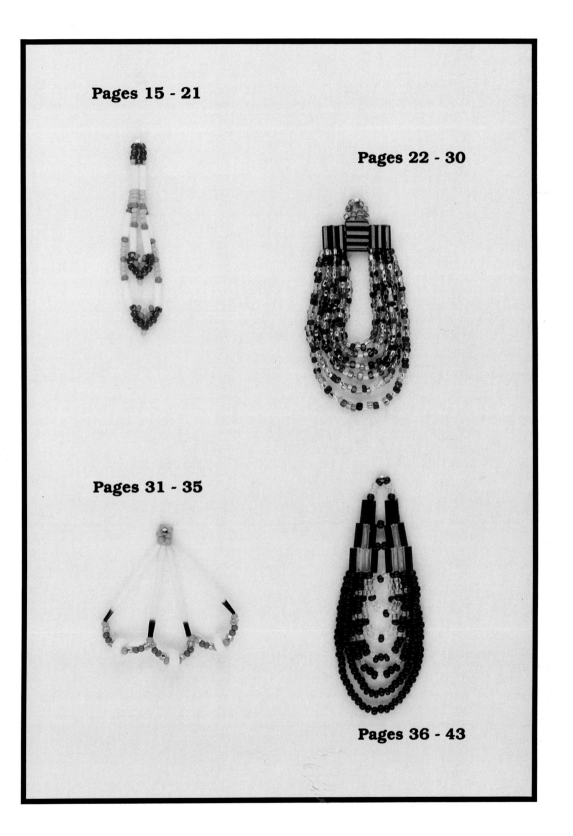

Pages 15 - 21

Pages 22 - 30

Pages 31 - 35

Pages 36 - 43

PLATE I

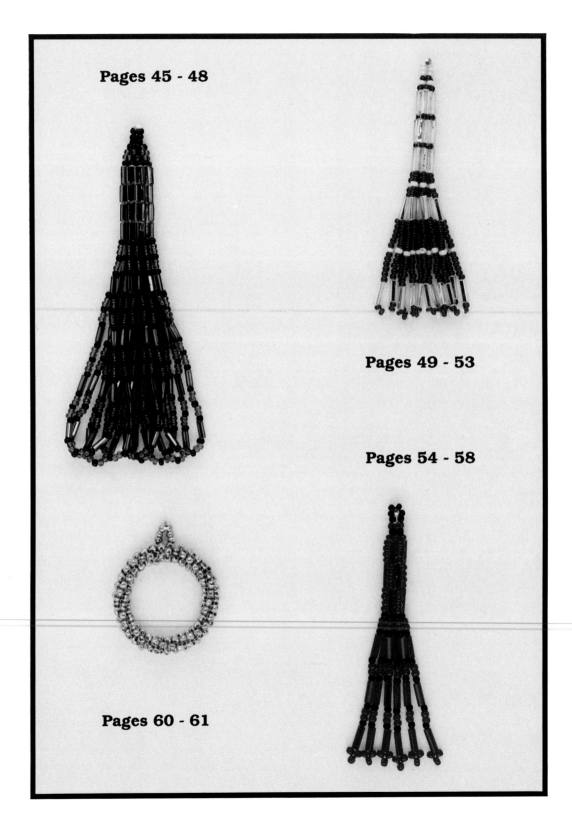

Pages 45 - 48

Pages 49 - 53

Pages 54 - 58

Pages 60 - 61

PLATE II

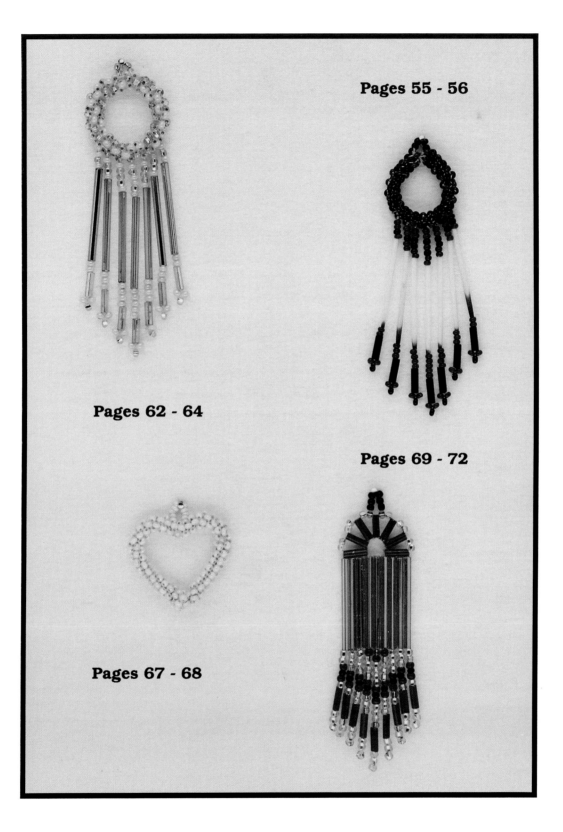

Pages 55 - 56

Pages 62 - 64

Pages 69 - 72

Pages 67 - 68

PLATE III

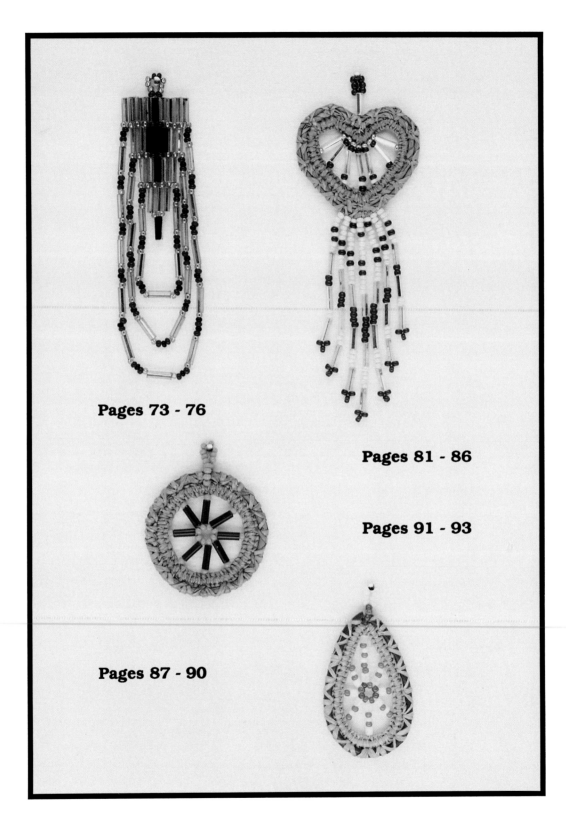

Pages 73 - 76

Pages 81 - 86

Pages 91 - 93

Pages 87 - 90

PLATE IV

BUGLE & SEED BEAD EARRINGS

Materials Required

Size O or A Nymo Thread
Size 15 Beading Needle
Size 3/0 Bugle Beads
Size 11/° Seed Beads
Round Toothpick
Large Cork
Clear Fingernail Polish

Please Note: The circumference of round toothpicks may vary but, in order to keep away from a great deal of repetition just to account for every difference in size, this project assumes that it will require six bugle beads to go around the toothpick. As you do this project, if you find that it takes only five bugle beads or seven of them, be sure and make that adjustment throughout the work. Further, as there are a great many similarities between this project and the last one, a reading of that project may be helpful.

Step 1. Using a thread measuring 1 1/2 yards in length, make a bugle bead foundation that is six bugle beads in length (see Introduction or any of the earlier projects for instructions on making a bugle bead foundation). As the work on this foundation progresses, periodically hold the foundation beads around a round toothpick; the length of the foundation should be just enough to go around so that the two end beads touch one another. This will be the first set. When the length is just right, go back though the bugle beads for added strength.

Step 2. As shown in Figure 1, attach five seed beads on the top of the bugle beads; this technique is described in the Introduction and in Step 1 on Page 45.

Figure 1

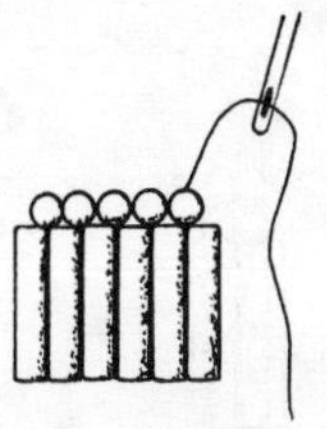

Figure 2

49

Turn the work over and, using the same technique, attach four seed beads. Then turn the work over and attach three seed beads. When this top row has been completed, as shown in Figure 2, thread on six seed beads. Take the needle down the first seed bead (to be used as an anchor bead on the left side), then go back up through the six seed beads and through the right side end seed bead (Figure 3). Continue taking the needle down each end seed bead and the end bugle bead on the right side.

Figure 3

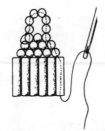

Step 3. With the thread coming down out of the last (Number 6) bugle bead, take the needle up through the first bugle bead (Number 1) thereby bringing both end bugle beads together. Pass the needle down the sixth bugle bead and back up the first as shown in Figure 4. Take the needle up the right side end bugle bead, up through the

Figure 4

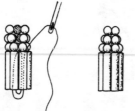

end seed bead, then over and down through the left end seed bead pulling the beads together. Repeat this process for the end seed beads of the remaining two rows, pulling the seed bead ends together. Tie a looped knot at a junction thread and finish off by threading both the needle and end

threads through the work and cutting off close to the work.

Step 4. Put a toothpick in the center of a large cork and place the beaded piece on the top of the toothpick as illustrated in Figure 5.

Figure 5

Step 5. Using a new thread 1 1/2 yards long, make another six bugle bead foundation. Go back through the work for added strength. Now attach five seed beads, as shown in Figure 1. When the last seed bead has been placed, take the needle down the end bugle bead (Figure 6). Now, with

Figure 6

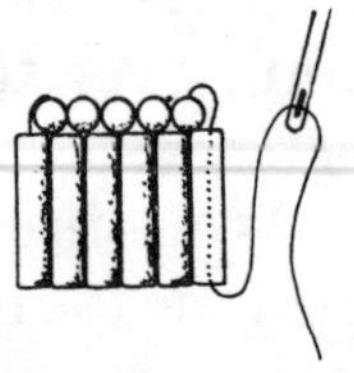

the same technique, attach five seed beads (Figure 7). Take the needle down the end bugle bead, then up through the other end bugle bead, bringing the ends together and forming a circle. Make another pass between these two end bugle beads to strengthen the work.

50

Figure 7

Figure 9

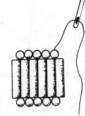

Step 6. There will be a space on the top and bottom sets of seed beads. In order to fill this space, take the needle up through one of the end seed beads, thread on one seed bead, then pass the needle under the junction thread (between the end bugle beads), then back up through the seed bead just threaded on. Take the needle over and down through the seed bead on the other side and down through the end bugle bead on that side. Turn the work over and repeat this step to fill in the space between the seed beads at this end (Figure 8). Pass the needle down one of the bugle beads and tie a looped knot at the junction thread. Finish off the thread in the usual manner. Place this set on the toothpick underneath the first set.

Figure 8

Step 8. With a new thread measuring 2 1/2 yards in length, pass the needle up and through the bottom section of one of the bugle beads leaving a six inch tail end thread, continue passing the needle through a bugle bead of the middle section (do not go through the seed beads), and up through a bugle bead in the top section. This will line up all of the sections. Do not take the needle through the seed beads at the top. Take the needle over and down through the

Step 7. Using a new thread measuring 1 1/2 yards long, make another six bugle bead foundation without the addition of the seed beads. Go back through the foundation for added strength. Then, as above, bring the end bugle beads together to form a circle and finish off the threads in the usual manner. As shown in Figure 9, place this set on the toothpick underneath the second set.

Figure 10

next bugle bead and go through the bugle beads beneath it. Bypass the seed beads of the middle section. Tie the tail end thread and the needle thread together in an overhand knot at the bottom (Figure 10).

Figure 11

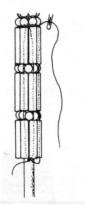

Step 9. As shown in Figure 11, take the needle up the next bugle bead and continue going up and down all sets until they are all aligned and attached. The thread should end up at the bottom of the work.

Step 10. Attach the dangle in the following manner: With the thread coming down and out of one of the bugle beads in the bottom foundation, thread on five seed beads, one bugle bead (junction), thirteen seed beads, one bugle bead, five seed beads, one bugle bead, thirteen seed beads, then go back through the first junction bugle bead and the five top seed beads. After the first dangle is threaded on, go back up the bugle beads in all foundation sets (as if it were one long bugle bead, bypassing again the seed beads). Now go over and down the next line in the same manner and thread on the next dangle. Repeat this Step until all the dangles are completed. Put the needle on the tail end thread and work it through the bead work, then clip it off. Finish the needle thread in the same manner.

Finishing: Liberally brush clear fingernail polish over the entire cylinder only. Twist the work on the toothpick without touching the cylinder so that it does not dry and stick to the toothpick. Allow it to dry completely before removing from the tooth pick.

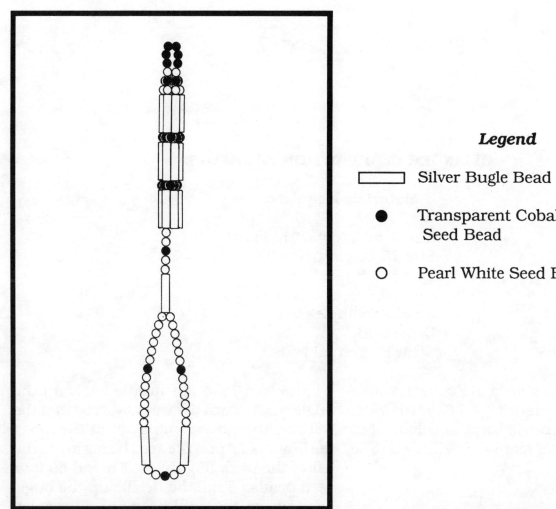

Legend

 Silver Bugle Bead

● Transparent Cobalt Blue
Seed Bead

○ Pearl White Seed Bead

CYLINDER COMBINATION EARRINGS

Materials Required

Size O or A Nymo Thread
Size 15 Beading Needle
Size 3/0 Bugle Beads
Size 10/° Seed Beads
Round Toothpick
Large Cork
Clear Fingernail Polish

Step 1. As shown in Figure 1, with a single thread measuring 1 1/2 yards long, thread on one bugle bead and four seed beads (or however many or few it takes to be

Figure 1

equal in length with the bugle bead). Take the needle back up the bugle bead, down through the seed beads and tie a knot with the tail end thread and the needle thread

Figure 2

(Figure 2). Take the needle back up the bugle bead. Turn the work over, so that the working thread is coming out at the top of the bugle bead and the seed beads are to the left of the work (Figure 3). Thread on four seed beads. Take the needle up the bugle bead, down the seed beads just threaded on, then thread on one more bugle bead. Continue in this fashion until there are three bugle beads and three sets of four seed beads as illustrated in Figure 4.

Figure 3

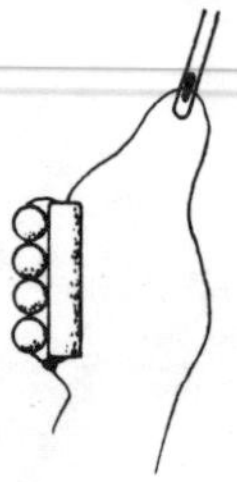

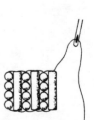

Figure 4

Step 2. Take the needle back through the work for added strength. As shown in the Introduction and in Step 1 on Page 49, at the top of the foundation created in Step 1 (above) add a row of five seed beads. Then turn the work and using the same technique, attach four seed beads. Turn the work and attach three seed beads. In order to make the ear wire loop (Figure 5), with the thread coming out of the top of the last (right side) top seed bead, thread on six seed beads. Then go down through the end seed bead on the left side, go back up through the six seed beads for added strength and then through the right side end seed bead.

Figure 5

Step 3. Go down the end bugle bead (right side) and up the first set of four seed beads (left side), forming a circle by bringing the two ends together. As shown in Figure 6, make another pass between these

Figure 6

two ends. Make sure the thread is coming up and out of the seed beads. Figure 7 illustrates how to take the needle up the end seed bead in the five seed bead row, then over and down through the seed bead at the other end of this same row. Repeat this step for strength and then go up through the end seed bead in the four seed bead row above. Repeat this circular work through the end seed beads of each row so that, as shown in Figure 8, they are all pulled

Figure 8

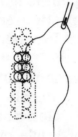

together, forming a cone shape. Tie a knot at a junction, go back through the beads and clip off any excess thread close to the work. Finish off the tail end thread in the same manner. Put this piece on top of a toothpick and place the toothpick in the center of the cork.

Step 4. Create two more sets of foundations as explained and illustrated in

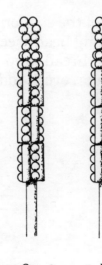

Figure 7   *Figure 9a*   *Figure 9b*

Step 1 but this time do not add the seed beads to the top. Bring the ends together to form a ring and finish off the threads in the usual manner. Slip these pieces on the toothpick below the first set. As shown in Figure 9, the sets may be alternated to achieve a "checkered" effect (9a) or lined up with the seed beads and bugle beads directly under one another (9b).

Step 5. Using a new thread measuring 2 1/2 yards in length, take the needle up through the bottom section of any bugle or seed bead set leaving a six inch tail end thread. Continue passing the needle up through the sections, lining them up, but do not take the needle through the seed beads at the top. Go over and down through the next set of bugle or seed beads and

Figure 10

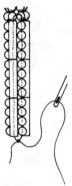

down through all of the sections beneath it as if it were one long bead (see Figure 10). Tie the tail end thread and the needle thread together in an overhand knot at the bottom. Continue with the needle up and down all of the sets until they are attached and lined up. The thread should be on the bottom of the work when complete. Place a needle on the tail end thread and work it back through the bead work to be clipped off close to the work.

Step 6. With the thread coming down out of the work, begin adding the dangles in the following manner: Thread on four seed beads, one bugle bead, four seed beads, one bugle bead, four seed beads, one bugle bead (junction) and three seed beads. Then go back through the last (junction) bugle bead and continue back through all of the beads in the dangle. Continue up through all of the beads in the three foundations (not the top seed beads) and then back down through the beads to the right. With the thread coming down and out of that row add another dangle as described in this Step. When all of the desired dangles are in place, tie a knot between any two beads in the body of the work, go through the work and then clip off any excess thread close to the earring.

Finishing: Liberally brush only the cylinder (body) of the earring with clear fingernail polish. Turn the work occasionally without touching the cylinder part as it dries so that it will not stick to the toothpick. Allow the work to dry overnight.

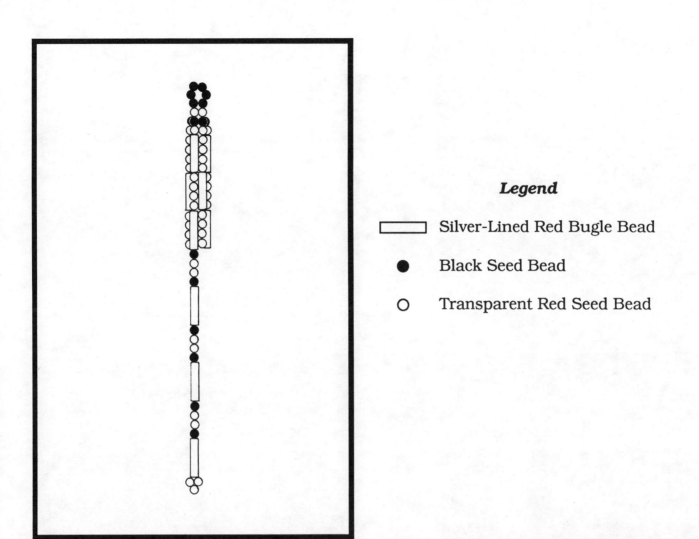

Legend

▭ Silver-Lined Red Bugle Bead

● Black Seed Bead

○ Transparent Red Seed Bead

NOTES

PEYOTE DESIGNS

PEYOTE STITCH

General Instructions

Step 1. Using a thread that is 2 1/2 yards in length, thread on the required number of beads. Go back through them again forming a loop or foundation row as shown in Figure 1. Tie a knot between the tail end thread and the needle thread.

Figure 1

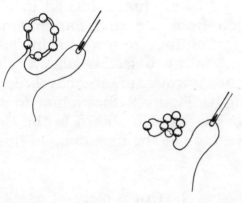

Figure 2

Step 2. Thread one seed bead on the needle thread and, skipping the foundation bead near it, take the needle through the next foundation bead (Figure 2). Continue threading on one seed bead, skipping one and going through the next. This technique will create a small space in which the next row of beads will fit (Figure 3) and will force the bead skipped in the foundation row to go down a bit.

Step 3. When the first bead in this row is reached, go through it, thread on one

Figure 3

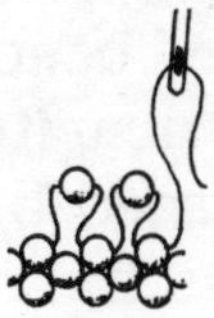

Figure 4

seed bead, then go through the next bead as shown in Figure 4. Continue in this manner until the desired length is reached. Take the needle, or working, thread back through the last row of beads threaded on to strengthen the end of the work.

59

PEYOTE CIRCLE EARRINGS

Materials Required

Size O or A Nymo Thread
Size 15 Beading Needle
Size 10/° Seed Beads
32 Gauge Thread Covered Wire
Clear Fingernail Polish
Needle Nose Pliers
Wire Cutters

Step 1. Using a thread measuring 2 1/2 yards long, thread on four seed beads. Thread through them again, forming a ring (these will be the foundation seed beads). Tie the tail end thread and the working thread together in an over hand knot. Thread on one seed bead, then skip the foundation seed bead near it and put the needle through the next seed bead. Thread on one seed bead, pass the next foundation seed bead and put the needle through the next foun-

dation bead as shown in Figure 1. Push the two seed beads just attached in a down position from the ring foundation seed beads. Continue to work in this fashion, working with two seed beads every round until the work measures exactly three inches in length. Figure 2 shows how to work a round; this is also shown in the General Instructions at the beginning of this Section.

Step 2. Cut a piece of wire 3 3/4" long. Pass this wire through the bead work and pull the end out with the pliers. Twist the ends of the wire together so that they cross. Push the ends of the peyote stitch work back, squeezing the ends of the wire

Figure 1

Figure 3

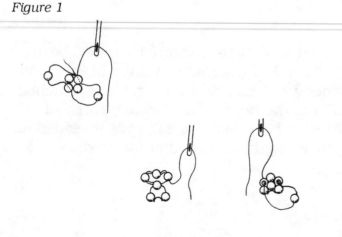

● - *Anchor Beads*

Figure 2

down, and then push the ends of the bead-work back over them. With the working thread, pass the needle back and forth from each end bead, bringing the ends close together. Tie a knot at a junction with the needle thread but do not cut it.

Figure 4

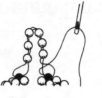

Step 3. Put a needle on the tail end thread and work through the bead work, then clip off any excess thread close to the work. Lining up the top beads of both sides (Figure 3), take the needle through the beads to reach one of the anchor beads. Go through this anchor bead and thread on six seed beads. Go over to the other anchor bead, through it and back up through the six seed beads, then through the other side of the beginning anchor bead (Figure 4). Work the thread through a junction thread, tie a knot and work through the bead work, then clip off close.

Finishing: Insure that the earring forms a perfect circle. Brush clear finger-nail polish over the entire top surface of this circle and allow to dry over night for a solid setting.

Legend

O   Silver Seed Bead

SMALL CIRCLE WITH LARGE BUGLE BEAD EARRINGS

Materials Required

Size O or A Nymo Thread
Size 15 Beading Needle
Size 3/0 Bugle Beads
Size 10/° Seed Beads
7/8" Long Bugle Beads
Clear Fingernail Polish

Step 1. Using a thread that is 2 1/2 yards long, begin by threading on four seed beads. Thread through again, making a loop (foundation). Tie the tail end thread and the working thread together in a knot. Thread on one seed bead, skip one seed bead of the foundation loop, and put the needle through the next seed bead. Push the two seed beads just attached in a downward position from the foundation. Continue to work in this fashion, working with two seed beads each round (see the General Instructions at the beginning of the Section) until the work, when bent around, will touch each other forming a tight natural circle with beads lined up as much as possible. Make this piece 2" in length.

Step 2. Pull the ends together, making sure that the seed beads form four columns, as shown in Figure 1. Take the needle through the end beads, back and forth to secure both ends tightly. Tie a knot at a junction and pass the needle through an anchor bead at the top (see Figure 2). Thread on six seed beads, go over to the next anchor bead, pass through it and back through the six seed beads, over and through the other side of the beginning anchor bead. Thread through a junction and tie a knot, then work through more beads and

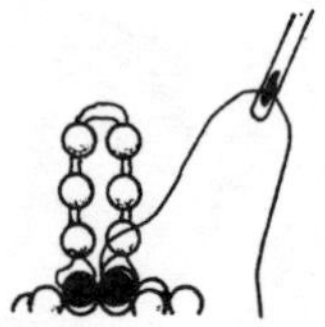

Figure 1

Figure 2

62

clip off the excess. Repeat this with the tail end thread.

Step 3. Take a look at the circle. Eye the center-bottom portion and pick a point on the left side (beginning) and a point on the right side (end) where the dangles will

Figure 3

• - *Anchor Beads*

be evenly spaced when placed along the bottom (see Figure 3). Using a new thread 2 1/2 yards long, tie a looped knot at the junction thread nearest the beginning anchor bead. Put a needle on the tail end thread, work it back through the bead work and clip off any excess. Pass the needle thread through the beginning anchor bead (left side) and, in order to make the first dangle, thread on three seed beads, one bugle bead, two seed beads, one bugle bead (junction bead), three seed beads, then go back up through the junction bugle bead and continue up through the rest of the dangle. After threading up through the beginning anchor bead, take the needle over to the next anchor bead to the right and proceed to make another dangle.

Figure 4

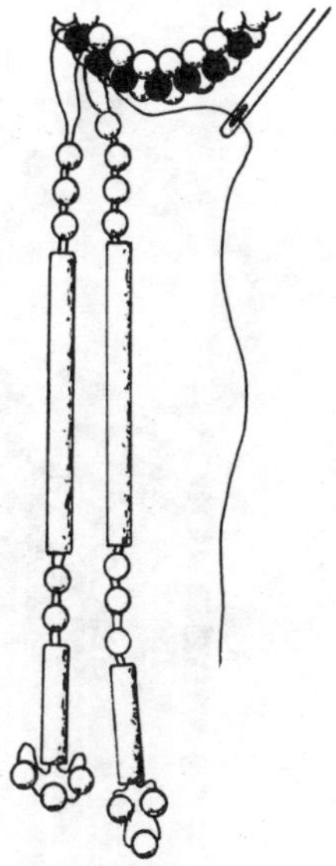

Continue in this fashion until all of the dangles are in place. Keep in mind that this, and other earrings, may be made unique by using different styles of dangles. A few are illustrated in the Introduction.

Finishing: Take the needle thread through some of the bead work, tie a knot at a junction, then go through some more bead work and clip off any excess thread. Insure that the earring forms a perfect circle and then brush clear fingernail polish over the entire front. Leave it overnight to set correctly.

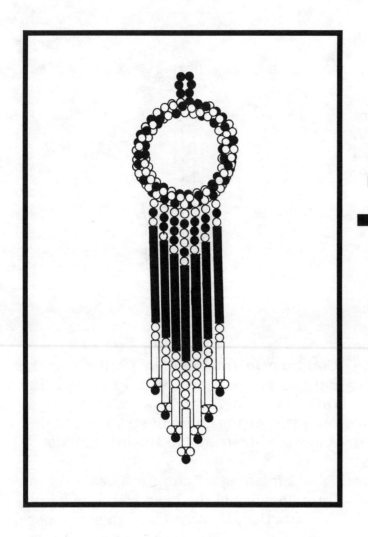

Legend

☐   Pink Bugle Bead

█   Gold Bugle Bead

●   Silver-Lined Gold Seed Bead

○   Pink Seed Bead

SMALL CIRCLE WITH QUILLS EARRINGS

Materials Required

Size O or A Nymo Thread
Size 15 Beading Needle
Size 3/0 Bugle Beads
Size 11/° Seed Beads
1" Porcupine Quills
Clear Fingernail Polish

Step 1. Using a thread that is 2 1/2 yards long, begin by threading on four seed beads. Thread through again making a loop (foundation). Tie the tail end thread and the working thread together in a knot. Thread on one seed bead, skip one seed bead of the foundation loop, and put the needle through the next seed bead. Push the two seed beads just attached in a downward position from the foundation. Continue to work, alternating colors (or use the same color) every two seed beads a round (see the General Instructions at the beginning of the Section) until the work, when bent around, will touch each other forming a tight natural circle with beads lined up as much as possible. Make this piece 2" in length.

Step 2. Pull the ends together, making sure that the seed beads form four columns, as shown in Figure 1 (they will twist slightly). Take the needle through the end beads, back and forth to secure both ends tightly. Tie a knot at a junction and pass the needle through an anchor bead at the top (see Figure 1). Thread on six seed beads, go over to the next anchor bead, pass through it and back through the six seed beads, over and through the other side of the beginning anchor bead. Thread through a junction and tie a knot, then work through more beads and clip off the excess. Repeat this with the tail end thread.

Step 3. Take a look at the circle. Eye the center-bottom portion and pick a point on the left side (beginning) and a point on the right side (end) where the dangles will

Figure 1

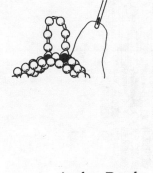

● - *Anchor Beads*

Figure 2

be evenly spaced when placed along the bottom (see Figure 2). Using a new thread 2 1/2 yards long, tie a looped knot at the junction thread nearest the beginning anchor bead. Put a needle on the tail end thread, work it back through the bead work and clip off any excess. Pass the needle thread through the beginning anchor bead (left side) and, in order to make the first dangle, thread on three seed beads, one porcupine quill, two seed beads, one bugle bead (junction bead), three seed beads and then go back up through the junction bugle bead and continue up through the rest of the dangle. After threading up through the beginning anchor bead, take the needle over to the next anchor bead to the right and proceed to make another dangle. Continue in this fashion until all of the dangles are in place.

Finishing: Take the needle thread through some of the bead work, tie a knot

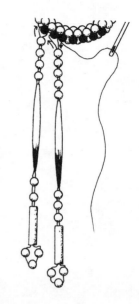

Figure 3

at a junction, then go through some more bead work and clip off any excess thread. Insure that the earring forms a perfect circle and then brush clear fingernail polish over the entire front. Leave it over night to set correctly.

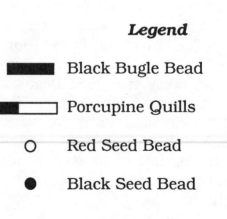

Legend

▬ Black Bugle Bead

▬▭ Porcupine Quills

○　Red Seed Bead

●　Black Seed Bead

PEYOTE HEART EARRINGS

Materials Required

Size O or A Nymo Thread
Size 15 Beading Needle
Size 11/° Seed Beads
32 Gauge Thread Covered Wire
Needle Nose Pliers
Wire Cutters
Clear Fingernail Polish

Step 1. Using a thread that is 2 1/2 yards long, begin by threading on four seed beads. Thread through again making a loop (foundation). Tie the tail end thread and the working thread together in a knot. Thread on one seed bead, skip one seed bead of the foundation loop, and put the needle through the next seed bead. Push the two seed beads just attached in a downward position from the foundation. Continue to work in this fashion, working with two seed beads every round (see the General Instructions at the beginning of this Section). Make this piece exactly 3 1/2" long.

Figure 1

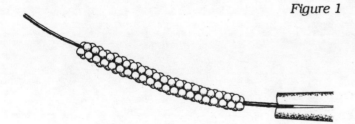

Step 2. Cut a piece of wire 4 1/4" long. Pass the wire through the bead work and pull the end out with the pliers (Figure 1). Twist the ends together so that they cross, as shown in Figure 2, and the peyote stitches are close to the twist. Clip off any excess wire, then push the ends of the peyote stitch work back, squeezing the ends of the wire down, then push the ends of the bead work back over them. With the working thread, pass the needle back and forth from each end bead, bringing the ends close together. Tie a knot at a junction with the working thread; this point then becomes the bottom point of the heart. Work the needle through a few beads and clip off any excess. Repeat this with the tail end thread.

Figure 2

Step 3. Form the bead work into a heart shape by pushing down the top mid-center and then squeezing in the sides. When formed into a nice shape, take a new thread that is 1 yard long and pass the needle through a junction thread near the top making a looped knot. Take the needle through the work up close to a matching point between the shoulders of the heart top (Figure 3). Thread on six seed beads for the ear wire loop, connect to an anchor bead on the other side, then go back through the six beads for strength and work through some of the bead work. Tie a knot and continue through some of the work, then clip off any excess thread.

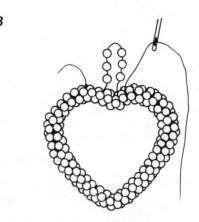

Figure 3

Finishing: Brush clear fingernail polish over the entire top surface of the heart and allow to dry overnight.

DECO DESIGNS

FAN & RECTANGLE EARRINGS

Materials Required

Size O or A Nymo Thread
Size 15 Beading Needle
Size 3/0 Bugle Beads
Size 10/° Seed Beads
7/8" Long Bugle Beads
Super Glue
Clear Fingernail Polish

Figure 2

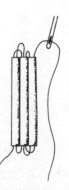

Step 1. With a 2 1/2 yard long thread, and working on a flat surface, thread on two large bugle beads. Lay them down on a flat surface, side by side. Then, take the needle up the first bugle bead and back down the second bugle bead, keeping them tight together and flat on the working surface as shown in Figure 1. This will keep the thread from stretching and breaking. Thread on a third bugle bead, lay it down beside the second bugle bead, then take the

Figure 1

needle down the second bugle bead and up the third (Figure 2). Keep the work flat and close together while attaching the next six bugle beads in the usual bugle bead foundation technique. There are nine bugle beads in this foundation. Thread back through the foundation for added strength.

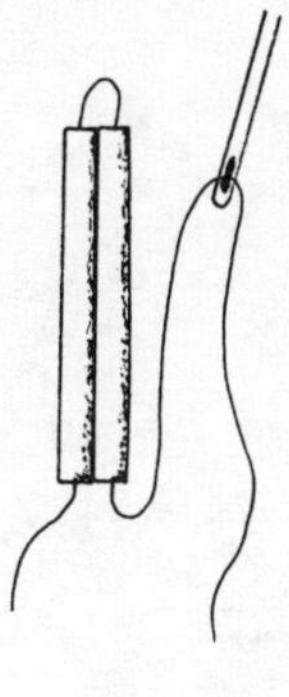

Step 2. Turn the work upside down, so that the working thread is now at the bottom and to the left. Place a needle on the

tail end thread, tie a looped knot at a junction, then work back through the bead work and clip off any excess thread close to the work.

Step 3. With the working thread at the bottom left side, the dangles may be created. Thread on six seed beads, one bugle bead and three seed beads. Take the needle back up the strand from the second seed bead up (Figure 3). Go up the large left-hand bugle bead in the foundation row,

Figure 3

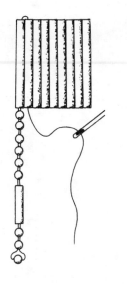

then over and down through the second large bugle bead. Thread on the remaining eight dangles in a similar fashion. When finished, the thread should be at the top of the right side bugle bead in the foundation. Take the needle to a junction thread and make a looped knot. Now proceed down the right-hand bugle bead and a few beads in the dangle, then clip it off close to the bead work.

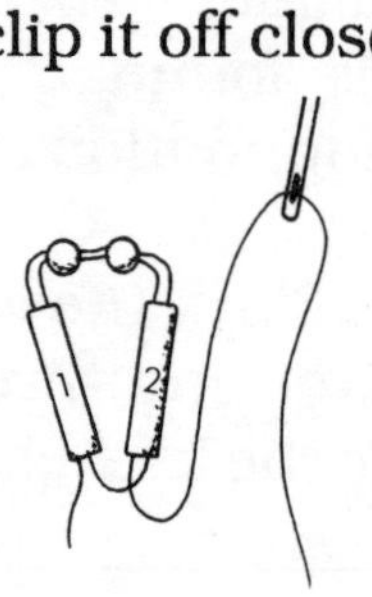

Figure 4

Step 4. With a new thread measuring 2 1/2 yards in length, thread on one bugle bead, two seed beads and one bugle bead. As shown in Figure 4, take the needle back through the first bugle bead, over and through the two seed beads and down the second bugle bead. Thread on one bugle bead, two seed beads and take the needle down the second bugle bead and up the third bugle bead (Figure 5). Thread on two seed beads and one bugle bead. Take the needle up the third bugle bead, over and

Figure 5

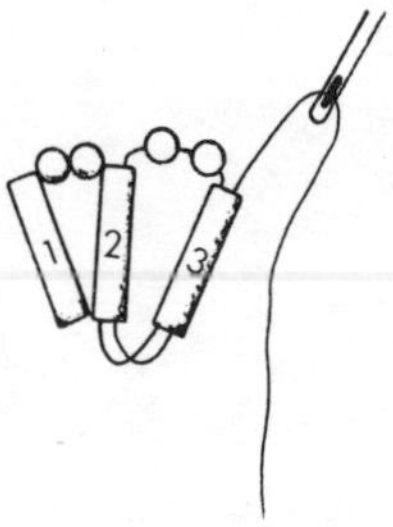

through the two seed beads and down the fourth bugle bead. Continue in this fashion until there are 7 bugle beads in the piece. Take the needle back through for added strength. Tie a knot between the tail end thread and the working thread. Put a needle on the tail end thread, then work it through the bead work and clip off any excess close to the work. Take the working thread up the first bugle bead.

Step 5. Take the needle over and through the two seed beads (left side), down the second bugle bead, up the third, over

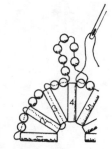

Figure 6

70

and through the two seed beads. Thread on six seed beads for the ear wire. As shown in Figure 6, take the needle through the first seed bead past the fourth bugle bead and use it as an anchor bead. Go back through the six seed beads, over and through the seed bead on the left of the fourth bugle bead (as in the anchor bead technique), as shown in Figure 7. Take the needle, as

Figure 7

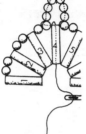

illustrated in Figure 8, down the fourth bugle bead, up the fifth bugle bead, over and through the two seed beads, down the sixth bugle bead and up through the seventh bugle bead.

Figure 8

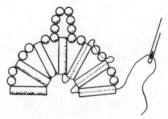

Step 6. Place the fan just created on top of the rectangle (large bugle bead foundation) created before. Take the needle down through the large bugle bead at the right side (bugle bead Number 9). Go up through the eighth bugle, down the seventh and then up the sixth large bugle bead (do not go through the dangles). Take the needle back through the seventh bugle bead of the fan (Figure 9). Take the needle back down the ninth large bugle bead in the foundation. This secures one end of the fan

Figure 9

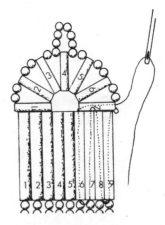

to the foundation. Work the thread up and down the large bugle bead foundation over and up the fourth bugle bead. Take the needle through the first bugle bead of the fan and back down the first large bugle bead of the foundation. Go up the second large bugle bead, down the third, up the fourth and back through the first bugle bead of the fan. Now, go back down the first large bugle bead. Make a loop knot on the bottom between the first and second large bugle bead just above the dangle. Take the needle back up the second 7/8" bugle bead, then clip off any excess thread.

Finishing: Lay the beadwork on a flat surface. Brush clear fingernail polish over the top of each of the two bead sections of the fan. Brush fingernail polish over the entire form of the large bugle bead foundation, including the first fan bugle bead and the seventh fan bugle bead (the ones that are attached to the large bugle bead foundation). Carefully apply super glue around the bugle bead ends that form a half-circle inside the bottom of the fan. Allow this to dry and then turn it over and apply clear fingernail polish to the large bugle bead foundation. Allow to set overnight.

71

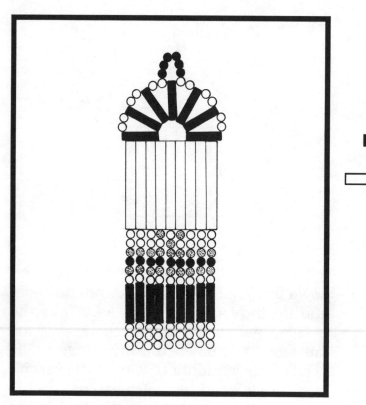

Legend

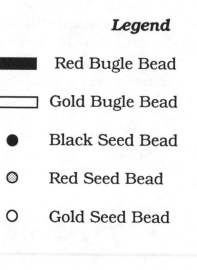

■	Red Bugle Bead
▭	Gold Bugle Bead
●	Black Seed Bead
◉	Red Seed Bead
○	Gold Seed Bead

TRIANGLE REVERSE EARRINGS

Materials Required

Size O or A Nymo Thread
Size 15 Beading Needle
Size 3/0 Bugle Beads
Size 11/° Seed Beads
Clear Fingernail Polish

Step 1. With a thread measuring 2 1/2 yards long, make a bugle bead foundation of nine bugles. Go back through for strength. Attach one row of eight seed beads (see Page 9). Turn the work and, using the same technique, attach seven bugle beads. Continue alternating the seed bead rows and the bugle bead rows until there is one bugle bead attached at the top of the work (Figure 1). Take the thread down through the end seed bead (Figure 2). Continue to take the needle down through the appropriate beads as shown in Figure 3.

Figure 2

Figure 1

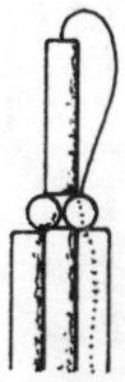

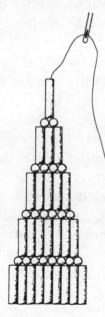

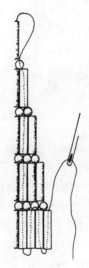

Figure 3

Step 2. As shown in Figure 4, turn the work so that the one bugle bead row is at the bottom and the thread is coming out of the first bugle bead of the first row on the left side. Thread on three seed beads and

Figure 4

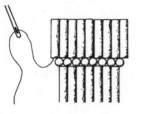

one bugle bead, then repeat this sequence thirteen times. Take the needle up the last right-hand bugle bead in the first (top) row (Figure 5). Now, take the needle down and

Figure 5

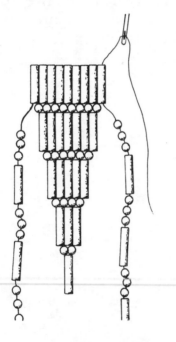

through the end bugle bead on the right side of the second row. As shown in Figure 6, thread on three seed beads and one bugle bead, repeat this four times, then thread on fifteen seed beads, then one bugle bead and three seed beads and repeat this four times again. Take the needle up the first bugle

bead on the left side of the second row of bugle beads. Take the needle down the second bugle bead of the second bugle bead row and down the first bugle bead of the third bugle bead row. Thread on three seed

Figure 6

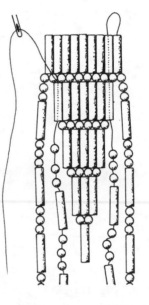

beads, one bugle bead, three seed beads, one bugle bead, fifteen seed beads, one bugle bead, three seed beads, one bugle bead and three seed beads. Take the needle up the end bugle bead (right side) of the third row of bugle beads.

Step 3. When the last dangle is complete, take the needle straight up all of the bugle beads to the top row. The needle should come up and out of the seventh bugle bead. Take the needle down the sixth bugle bead and up the fifth bugle bead (Figures 7 and 8). Pass the needle through the junction thread that is between the fourth and fifth bugle bead. Make a looped knot and thread on eight bugle beads. Take the needle over to the junction thread between the fifth and sixth bugle bead, make a looped knot, as shown in Figure 9. Go back through the eight seed beads for

74

Figure 7

Figure 9

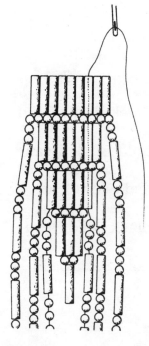

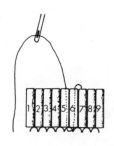

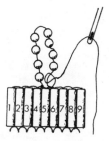

Figure 8

strength, make a knot at a junction, go through a few beads and clip off close to the work. Finish off the tail end thread in the same manner.

Finishing: Brush the entire surface of the triangle with clear fingernail polish and allow to dry overnight.

75

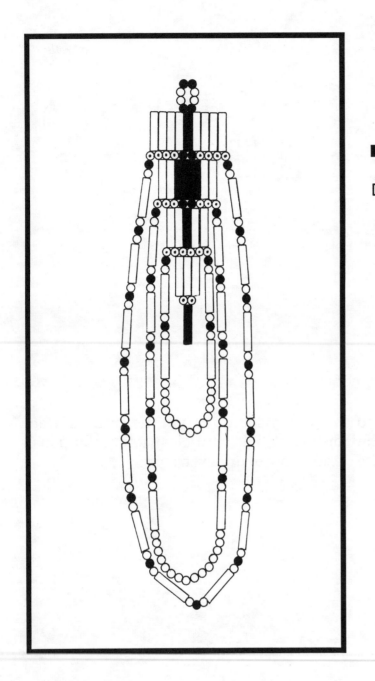

Legend

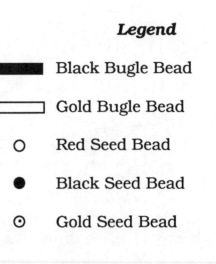

▬▬	Black Bugle Bead
▭	Gold Bugle Bead
○	Red Seed Bead
●	Black Seed Bead
⊙	Gold Seed Bead

76

PINE NEEDLE DESIGNS

PINE NEEDLE AND RAFFIA TECHNIQUES

All of the following projects in this book are made using the same basic instructions. They are described and illustrated here in order to reduce lengthy repetition in the individual project directions.

BASIC INSTRUCTIONS

Step 1. Using a 32 gauge wire, the wire is cut so that it is twice the length of the circumference required. This length allows the wire to be crossed at the top and the free wire ends twisted over itself (Figure 1). The

Figure 1

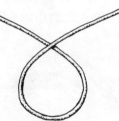

left free wire is twisted first and then, after the work is turned around, the twist on the right side (now on the left) as illustrated in Figures 2 and 3. The ends of the wire will meet at the bottom of the circle (Figure 4)

Figure 2

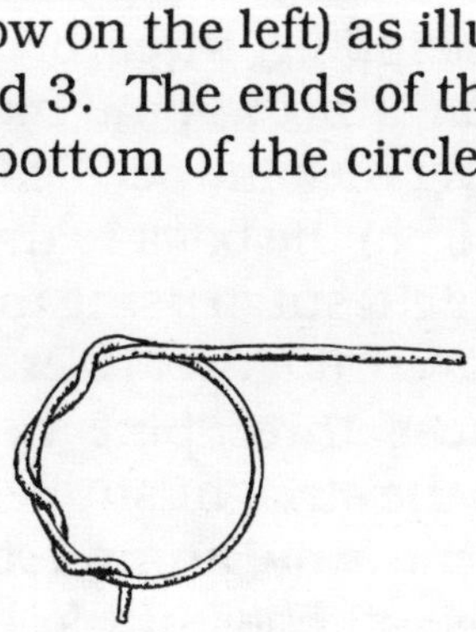

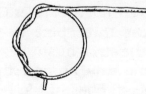

and the ends should be cut flush with the bottom and the sharp ends pushed in tight. *Figure 3*

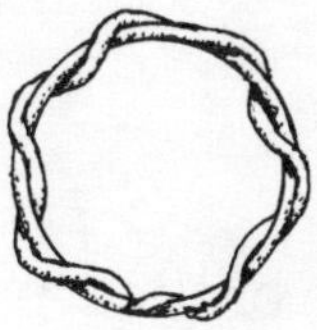

Figure 4

Step 2. When the wire shape has been completed and strengthened by twisting, the next step is to wrap the wire com-

Figure 5

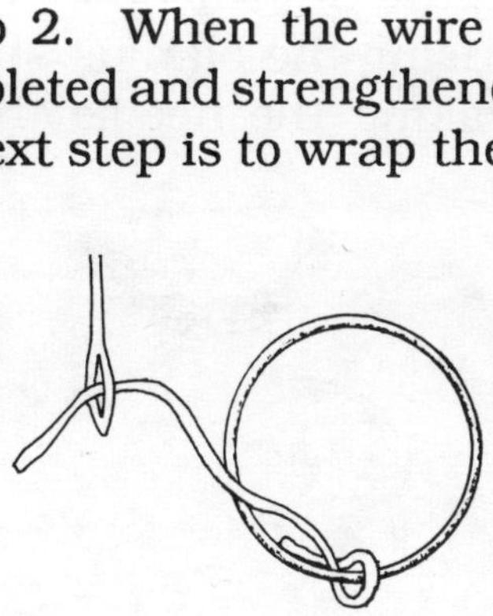

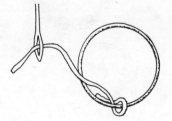

77

pletely with raffia, using the blanket stitch (Figures 5 and 6), and a crewel needle (the blanket stitch is also known as the button hole stitch). The raffia grass should be split lengthwise in half or fourths to get the

Figure 6

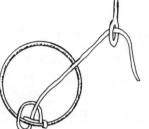

appropriate width. Begin by placing one inch of the raffia on the bottom center point of the wire, over the ends of the twisted portion. Make a loop and come up through it (Figure 6). This makes a complete blanket stitch (Figure 7). Continue making blanket stitches close together on the in-

Figure 7

side of the wire frame and work all the way around until the first stitch is reached. Take the raffia through it, locking them together (Figure 8). Turn the work around and begin using the blanket stitch again, this time taking the needle through the

Figure 8

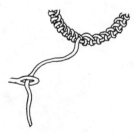

natural stitch holes created by the inner stitches (Figure 9). Continue all the way around and go through the first outer stitch to lock both together.

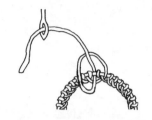

Figure 9

Step 3. This step explains the application of the pine needles and the special decorative stitch that holds them to the covered wire frame (and to each row of pine needles themselves if it should be desireable to add more than one row of pine needle work). These stitches shall all be made as tightly as possible without breaking the raffia. Keep in mind that pine needles will shrink slightly when drying. Just past where the raffia emerges from the last blanket stitch, place the blunt end of three pine needles. As shown in Figure 10, make a pass over the pine needles, bringing

Figure 10

the needle from the back to the front using the blanket stitch. Next make a slanting stitch by skipping three or four blanket stitches beneath the pine needles, taking the raffia over the pine needles and bringing the needle from the back to the front. Then make a straight stitch using the same stitch hole just used (Figure 10). Continue attaching these three pine needles to the frame with the straight stitch and the slant stitch all the way around the shape to within three stitches of the beginning. If only one row of work is to be done, cut the ends of the pine needles at a slant (to fit flush with the top of the work). This is illustrated in Figure 11. Then make the straight stitch and slant stitch to secure these ends and cover them. Finally, take the raffia back through a blanket stitch and go to the inside raffia stitches, go through six or seven inner stitches, pull tightly and cut off close to the work.

Figure 11

Step 4. If more than one row of pine needle work is desired, continue placing the three pine needles over the first row and make the slant stitch by passing the raffia over the pine needles and coming through the **center** of the straight stitch of the previous row from back to front. This splits the previous straight stitch (Figure 12). Bring the needle over the pine needles, take the needle from back to front and pull the raffia taut. This makes the straight stitch.

Figure 12

Continue in this manner all around, replacing the pine needles if necessary and finishing the pine needle ends as mentioned in Step 3, Figure 11. When the last stitch has been completed, reverse the direction and make only slant stitches all the way around,

Figure 13

using the center of the straight stitches (Figure 13). This not only adds decoration but serves to strengthen the work. Take the raffia back down to the first row of stitches, then down to the inner blanket stitches. Go over and up through six or seven blanket stitches, pull the raffia up tight and clip it off close to the work.

SPECIAL NOTES

Soaking Pine Needles: In order to use the pine needles, place them in a pan and pour scalding water over them. Allow them to sit for one hour then take them out and roll them in a damp towel. Let them sit for three hours until they are damp and flexible.

Adding New Pine Needles: Usually, in the following projects, the pine needles are long enough to go around the forms twice. The longest pine needles available should be selected for these earring designs. In the South, the needles from the Loblolly or Long Leaf Pine will work; in the West, those from the Coulter, Digger or Ponderosa pines are suitable. With the Ponderosa, three needles are held together by a pitchy bud and they are usually 6 inches or more in length. By clipping off the bud, there will be 3 single needles to use.

To add a needle to a project, simply slip the new pine needle slightly under the one in place and make a stitch to hold it taut.

Using New Raffia: After splitting the raffia lengthwise in half or in fourths, clip off the stiff ends and discard any that are too fine to use.

Finishing the Raffia: Weave the old

raffia strand back through the blanket stitches by going over and through each stitch. Pull the raffia up tightly and clip.

Tying on New Raffia: Choose the third or fourth stitch away from the place to be worked. Thread through a new strand of raffia and weave through the blanket stitches up to the place to be worked. After a few new stitches have been made (either in plain blanket stitch or working over the pine needles), go back to the tail end of the raffia, pull it up tightly and cut off the excess.

Avoiding Fraying: Remember to move the needle up the raffia strand often to avoid fraying. Further, instead of putting pressure on the raffia at the eye of the needle, pull the middle section of raffia instead when tightening the stitches.

PINE NEEDLE HEART EARRINGS

Materials Required

Pine Needles
4 Strands of 1/8" Raffia
Small Crewel Needle
Size O or A Nymo Thread
Size 15 Beading Needle
Size 3/0 Bugle Beads
Size 11/° Seed Beads
32 Gauge Thread Covered Wire
Needle Nose Pliers
Wire Cutters
Thimble

It is suggested that the Section before this one, covering the basics of working with pine needles and raffia, be read before attempting this project.

Step 1. With the wire cutters, cut a length of wire that measures seven (7") inches. Form the wire into a circle with a circumference of 1 1/4" (see Figure 1). Twist the ends of the wire over itself, first one side, then turn it over and complete the other side with both ends meeting at the bottom (Figure 2). Cut the ends flush to the bottom wire.

Figure 2

Figure 1

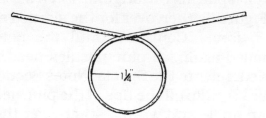

Figure 3

Step 2. Form the wire into a heart shape by pushing down the middle of the top of the circle, forming the shoulders of the hearts around the forefingers and then squeezing the sides in and down to a point where the wire ends meet (Figure 3).

Step 3. As illustrated in Figure 4, with a strand of raffia, using a crewel needle, begin wrapping the inside of the heart with

Figure 4

a blanket stitch (also called the "button hole" stitch). Lay the raffia, with a 1" tail end, on the wire form and make one stitch around the wire and over the end piece of the raffia. This will secure the raffia to the wire. Continue wrapping until the end piece is secured by six to eight stitches and clip off close to the last made stitch. With the needle raffia strand, continue wrapping the wire with the blanket stitch until reaching the first stitch. Take the raffia through this stitch, locking them together.

Step 4. Turn the work upside down so that the bottom of the heart is at the top and begin doing the outside of the heart with the blanket stitch using the inner stitch as the points through which to put the needle. Work to the left and go all around the shape. Pass the needle through the top of the first blanket stitch, thus locking them together. There should be three feet or more of raffia to continue the work. If there is less, finish off the old raffia and, as described in the Special Notes, add

a new strand.

Step 5. Beginning with the bottom point of the heart, place three pine needles on top of the form and pass the raffia over them pushing the needle from the back through to the front using the same hole (this is the blanket stitch on the outside of the heart), as shown in Figure 5. Skip three or four blanket stitches, take the raffia over

Figure 5

the pine needles, with the needle through the blanket stitch in back to front. Take the needle over the pine needles, again pushing the needle from the back through to the front in the same blanket stitch. Continue around the heart until the point is reached again.

Step 6. Go over the point to make a second row of pine needle work. This time bring the needle through the middle of the straight stitch from the back to the front, go over the pine needles, bring the raffia from

Figure 6

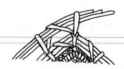

the back to the front through the same stitch (splitting the original stitch as shown in Figure 6), then over for the slanted stitch as before. Continue until the point is reached again. If pine needles need to be added, refer to the Special Notes Section on Page 79. Clip off the tips of the pine needles at an angle and wrap a stitch over them.

Step 7. As shown in Figure 7, go back over the work to create a crossing effect by making a slanting stitch to the right. Continue until the point of the heart is reached. Take the needle through the

Figure 7

Figure 9

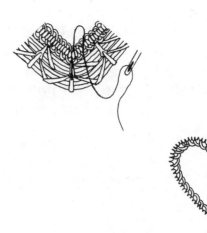

inside blanket stitch of the wire frame and weave in and out. Clip off any excess raffia. The heart is now ready for the bead work. The needle nose pliers may be used to push the beading needle through the pine needle work and the thimble may prove useful.

Step 8. Using a thread measuring 1 1/2 yards long, knot one end. As shown in Figure 8, from the back of the heart, at the point, push the needle through. Make a

Figure 8

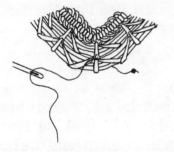

small running stitch from the front to the back. Now take the needle up to and through the inside blanket stitch at the point (Figure 9). As shown in Figure 10, thread on three seed beads, one bugle bead, three seed beads and take the needle up to and through the inner blanket stitch that is at the point between the shoulders of the heart. The inner blanket stitches will be

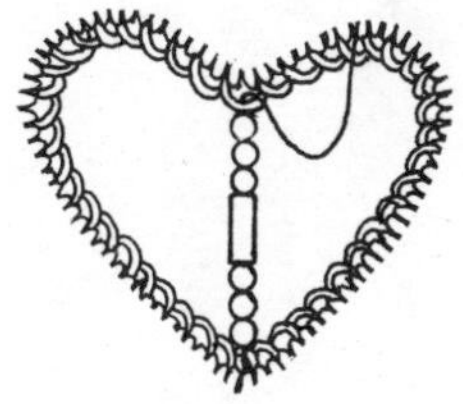

Figure 10

used as if they were anchor beads. Take the needle back down the beads just threaded on, back through the same bottom stitch and then back up the bead line again. Take the needle through the same stitch, then go

Figure 11

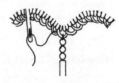

through the blanket stitch to the left of the first one (Figure 11). Thread on beads (as per the Diagram on Page 84) and go through the third or fourth blanket stitch to the left of the first center line of beads. Put the needle through this stitch and go back up the beads just threaded on. Go through the stitch, then come up and through the next blanket stitch to the left. Following the Diagram, repeat this process until the left side is done and the thread is coming up at the top of the last line. Weave the needle in and out of these top inner stitches, to the stitch to the right of the center line. Repeat, placing the bead work in place in the same manner, being careful that they match the same angles as on the left side.

Step 9. Now weave back and forth through the stitches to the center again. Put the needle up through the upper blanket stitch. Make a small running stitch through the pine needle work and come out

Figure 12

in the center (front) and between the two rows (see Figure 12). Form the ear wire loop by threading on eight seed beads. Pass the needle through the work from the other side (back side), coming out at the first seed bead. Thread the needle back through the eight seed beads for strength. Come out

Figure 13

where the beads began and go through the first four of them. Then thread on eight seed beads. Pass the needle under the loop (of previous seed beads) to the left and up through this new set of eight seed beads again forming a second loop (Figure 13). Make a knot and go back through the work, then cut off any excess thread close to the work.

One earring is now ready to wear, or, by following the option below, dangles may be added to it.

OPTIONAL DANGLES

This particular style of dangle may also be used for the Pine Needle Circle Earrings if desired.

Materials Required

Size O or A Nymo Thread
Size 15 Beading Needle
Size 3/0 Bugle Beads
Size 11/° Seed Beads

Step 1. Tie a knot in the end of a thread measuring 2 1/2 yards long. Thread on five seed beads, making sure that the knot is large enough to hold the beads at the bottom of the thread. Pass the needle

Figure 13

through the pine needle work, from back to front, then pass the needle up through the seed beads securing them on the bottom tip of the heart as shown in Figure 13.

Step 2. As shown in Figure 14, thread on four seed beads, pass the needle

Figure 14

from the back to the front of the pine needle work, near the first line of beads and back up the four seed beads. This can be either to the right side of the first five seed beads or to the left. Continue this process with one less bead until there is one bead left to work (Figure 15).

Figure 15

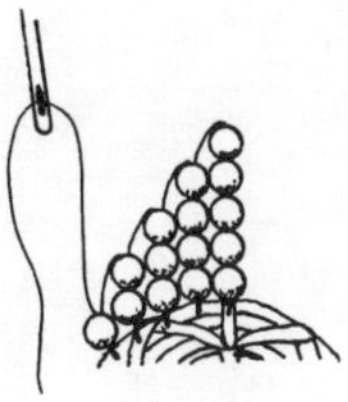

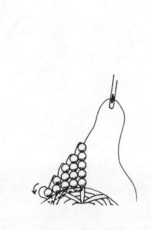

Figure 16

Step 3. Figure 16 illustrates taking the needle through the pine needle work right by the side of the last bead and making tiny running stitches back to the center five seed beads. Then take the needle back up through the five seed beads, thread on four

seed beads and repeat the process until the last bead is attached. Take the needle down close beside the last bead, going through the pine needles at an angle and then through the last bead once more. At this point the bead strands that make up the dangles will be attached (Figure 17).

Figure 17

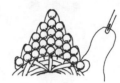

Step 4. Using Figure 18 as a guide, thread on the required number of beads for the first dangle. Come back up the bead strand in the dangle, through the first bead, take the needle over to the beginning of the two seed beads, through both of them and

Figure 18

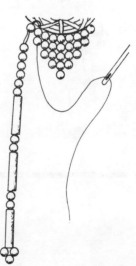

then thread on the required number of beads for the next dangle. Repeat this until the last seed bead is reached and the dangle is complete. Take the needle through the pine needle work. Tie a knot. Make tiny running stitches through the pine needles and clip off close to the work. Also, clip off the tail end tip from the knots if there are any.

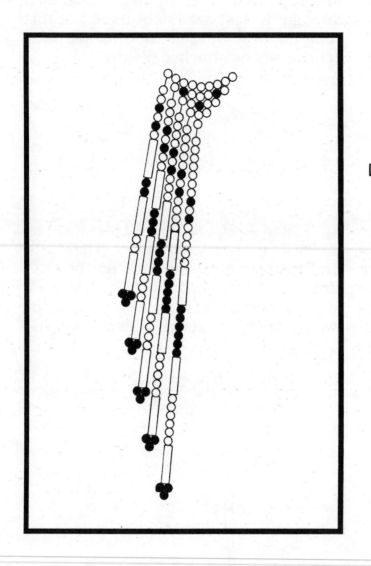

Legend

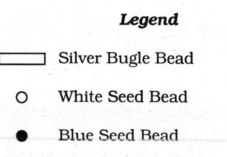

▭ Silver Bugle Bead

○ White Seed Bead

● Blue Seed Bead

PINE NEEDLE CIRCLE EARRINGS

Materials Required

Pine Needles
4 Strands of 1/8" Raffia
Small Crewel Needle
Size O or A Nymo Thread
Size 15 Beading Needle
Size 3/0 Bugle Beads
Size 10/° Seed Beads
32 Gauge Thread Covered Wire
Needle Nose Pliers
Wire Cutters
Thimble

It is suggested that the Section before the Pine Needle Heart Earrings, covering the basics of working with pine needles and raffia, be read before attempting this project.

Step 1. With the wire cutters, cut a length of wire that measures seven (7") inches. Form it into a circle with a circumference of 1 1/4". Twist the wire end over the circle shape, first one side, then turn the work and twist the other end wire so that both ends meet at the bottom (Figure 1). Cut the ends flush to the bottom wire.

Step 2. Thread a strand of raffia on the crewel needle. As shown in Figures 2 and 3, begin wrapping the inside of the circle with a blanket stitch. By laying 1" of the raffia strand end down on the wire form, make one blanket stitch over the wire and another stitch over the wire and raffia end

Figure 2

Figure 1

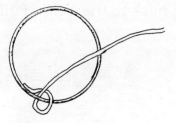

87

(Figure 3). Continue wrapping wire with this stitch until six or eight stitches have been completed and clip off the end of the raffia close to the last stitch. With the needle raffia strand, continue wrapping with the blanket stitch until the first stitch is reached; take the raffia through the top of

Figure 3

the first stitch thus locking them together.

Step 3. Turn the work so that the raffia strand is at the top and begin wrapping the outside of the wire with the blanket stitch using the inner stitch as the place through which the needle goes. Put the needle through the bottom loop of the blanket stitch, front to back, then through the loop previously made. Work to the left all the way around. Lock the end and the beginning stitch together as before.

Step 4. As shown in Figure 4, with each at an angle, place the three pine needles on top of the wrapped form. Pass the raffia over them, front to back, through the outer blanket stitches. Go through from the back to the front. Pull up tightly.

Figure 4

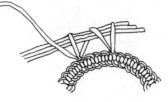

Skip three or four blanket stitches, then take the raffia over the pine needles, front to back, through a blanket stitch, back to front. Make a straight stitch in the same place. Continue until the beginning pine needles are reached.

Step 5. As the pine needles began at an angle, clip the ends of the pine needles to match the beginning and end of each pine needle, over-lapping them slightly. Make another straight wrapping stitch over the ends to secure them. Then, with the raffia in the front of the work, make a slanting stitch to the right, bringing the raffia from back to front, in front of a straight stitch (Figure 5). Continue all the

Figure 5

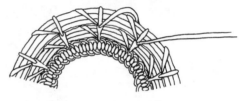

way around until the beginning point is reached. Take the raffia strand down to the inner blanket stitches. Weave the raffia through several stitches and pull up tightly. Clip off any excess. The earring is now ready for the bead work.

Step 6. Using a thread 2 1/2 yards in length, thread on eight seed beads, passing the needle through them again, forming a circle foundation. Tie a knot using the tail end thread and the needle thread. Leave the tail end thread to be worked later. Lay the pine needle circle down and place the beaded circle in the center. Judge how many seed and bugle beads it will take to reach and touch the inside raffia stitch. Thread on a bugle bead and then a seed bead and see how far it will go to meet the inner raffia blanket stitch. As shown in Figure 6, when sufficient beads have been threaded on, pass the needle through the blanket stitch and then back through the beads just threaded. Take the needle through the next four seed beads of the foundation. Add on the required number of

Figure 7

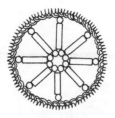

Figure 6

inner blanket stitch, from the back of the work to the front (Figure 8).

Step 8. After making sure that the bead design is centered, thread on eight

Figure 8

beads. Place the beads at a 6 o'clock position and attach through the appropriate blanket stitch, then back through the beads to the foundation. Take the needle through the next two beads, thread on the required number of beads, go through the blanket stitch at a 9 o'clock position and back down the beads. Thread through four foundation seed beads, thread on the requisite beads and attach at the 3 o'clock position. Put a needle on the tail end thread and take it up through a few beads. Cut off any excess thread close to the work.

Step 7. Take the needle thread through the next seed bead on the foundation and thread on the correct number of beads. Secure through the raffia blanket stitch and go back through the beads just threaded. Take the needle through the next two seed beads of the foundation and repeat until four more positions have been completed between the four previously done (see Figure 7). Take the needle through one more foundation seed bead. Tie the needle thread in a knot at a junction. Pass through a few beads. Take the needle through the

seed beads, pass the needle through the work from the back to the front, coming out at the first bead, and thread the needle back through the eight seed beads for strength. Pull the thread taut (Figure 9). The needle should now be in front. Go through the first four seed beads and thread on eight seed beads, passing the needle under the beaded loop and up through the left side of the new set of beads forming a second loop. Make a loop knot and go back through the remaining four seed beads and through the pine needle work. Clip off any excess thread close to the work.

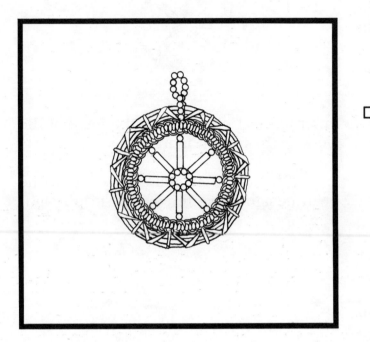

Legend

▭ Dark Blue Bugle Bead

O Turquoise Seed Bead

PINE NEEDLE TEAR DROP EARRINGS

Materials Required

Pine Needles
4 Strands of 1/8" Raffia
Small Crewel Needle
Size O or A Nymo Thread
Size 15 Beading Needle
Size 3/0 Bugle Beads
Size 11/° Seed Beads
32 Gauge Thread-
    Covered Wire
Needle Nose Pliers
Wire Cutters
Thimble

It is suggested that the Section before the Pine Needle Heart Earrings, covering the basics of working with pine needles and raffia, be read before attempting this project.

Step 1. With the wire cutters, cut a wire that measures 7" in length. Form it into a circle with a circumference of 1 1/4". Twist the wire end over the circle shape, first one side, then turn the work and twist the other end wire, so both ends meet at the bottom as shown in Figure 1. Cut the ends flush to the bottom wire, squeezing the sharp end into the form.

Step 2. Now, as shown in Figure 2, make a tear drop shape by pinching the top point of the circle together and pulling the bottom down until the tear drop shape is

Figure 1

Figure 2

91

complete.

Step 3. Thread a strand of raffia on the crewel needle. Begin wrapping the inside of the tear drop with a blanket stitch as shown in Figure 3. Continue wrapping with the blanket stitch until reaching the

Figure 3

first stitch, then take the raffia through the top of the stitch thus locking them both together.

Step 4. Begin wrapping the outside of the wire with the blanket stitch, using the inner stitches as the place to put the needle through. Put the needle through the bottom loop of the blanket stitch, front to back, then through the loop just made. Work to the left all the way around. Lock the end and beginning stitch together as before.

Step 5. Starting at the bottom of the tear drop, as shown in Figure 4, place the three pine needles on the wrapped form, each one at an angle. Pass the raffia over them, front over to the back, through the

Figure 4

outer blanket stitches. Go through the back to the front and pull up tightly. Skip three or four blanket stitches, then take the raffia over the pine needles, front to back, through a blanket stitch going back to front. Make a straight stitch in this same place. Continue alternating slanting and straight stitches until reaching the beginning pine needles. At this point, a choice can be made as to the number of rows of pine needles to be placed. If one row, continue to Step 6; if two, see the Basic Instructions on Page 79.

Step 6. As the pine needles began at an angle, clip the ends of the pine needles to match the beginning and end of each one leaving a slight overlap. Make a straight wrapping stitch over the ends to secure them. With the raffia at the front of the work, as shown in Figure 5, make a slanting stitch to the right, bring the raffia from the

Figure 5

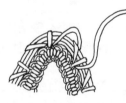

back to the front, in front of the previous straight stitch. Continue in this fashion to the beginning. Take the raffia strand down to the inner blanket stitches. Weave the raffia through several stitches and pull up taut. Clip up close to the work. The earring is now ready for the bead work phase.

Step 7. Using a thread that is 2 1/2 yards long, thread on eight seed beads, passing the needle through them again and forming a circle foundation. Tie a knot between the tail end thread and the needle or working thread. Leave the tail end thread to be worked later. Lay the pine needle tear drop down and place the beaded circle in the middle. Judge how many seed and bugle beads it will take to reach and touch the inside raffia blanket stitch. Thread on a bugle bead and then a seed bead and see how far it will go up to meet the raffia

Figure 7

Figure 6

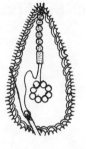

stitch at the top point of the tear drop. When sufficient beads have been threaded, pass the needle through the blanket stitch, then back through the beads just added (Figure 6). Take the needle through the next four seed beads of the foundation. Add the required number of beads. Place the beads at a 6 o'clock position and attach through the appropriate blanket stitch , then going back through the beads just put in place. Take the needle through the next two foundation seed beads. Thread on the required number of beads, go through the blanket stitch at a 9 o'clock position and back down the beads. Thread through four foundation seed beads, thread on beads, attach at the 3 o'clock position and go back through the beads (Figure 7). Put a needle on the tail end thread and take it up through a few beads before cutting off excess thread close to the work.

Step 8. Take the needle through the next seed bead on the foundation and thread on the required number of beads (see Figure 7). Secure through the raffia stitch and go back through the beads just added. Take the needle through the next two seed beads of the foundation and repeat until four positions have been completed between the four previously done. Take the needle through one more foundation seed bead. Tie a needle thread in a knot at a junction. Pass through a few beads and then clip off any excess close to the work. The earring loop is added as in the previous projects in this section (see Figure 8).

Figure 8

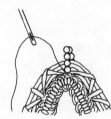

Legend

⊛　White Seed Bead

●　Orange Seed Bead

EAGLE'S VIEW BESTSELLERS

❑	**The Technique of Porcupine Quill Decoration**/Orchard	B00/01	$8.95
❑	In Hardback	B99/01	$15.95
❑	**The Technique of North American Indian Beadwork**/Smith	B00/02	$9.95
❑	In Hardback	B99/02	$15.95
❑	**Techniques of Beading Earrings** by Deon DeLange	B00/03	$7.95
❑	**More Techniques of Beading Earrings** by Deon DeLange	B00/04	$8.95
❑	**America's** *First* **First World War: The French & Indian**/Todish	B00/05	$8.95
❑	**Crow Indian Beadwork**/Wildschut and Ewers	B00/06	$8.95
❑	**New Adventures in Beading Earrings** by Laura Reid	B00/07	$8.95
❑	**North American Indian Burial Customs** by Dr. H. C. Yarrow	B00/09	$9.95
❑	**Traditional Indian Crafts** by Monte Smith	B00/10	$7.95
❑	**Traditional Indian Bead & Leather Crafts**/ Smith & VanSickle	B00/11	$8.95
❑	**Indian Clothing of the Great Lakes: 1740-1840**/Hartman	B00/12	$9.95
❑	In Hardback	B99/12	$15.95
❑	**Shinin' Trails: A Possibles Bag of Fur Trade Trivia** by Legg	B00/13	$7.95
❑	**Adventures in Creating Earrings** by Laura Reid	B00/14	$9.95
❑	**Circle of Power** by William F. Higbie	B00/15	$7.95
❑	In Hardback	B99/15	$13.95
❑	**Etienne Provost: Man of the Mountains** by Jack Tykal	B00/16	$9.95
❑	In Hardback	B99/16	$15.95
❑	**A Quillwork Companion** by Jean Heinbuch	B00/17	$9.95
❑	In Hardback	B99/17	$15.95
❑	**Making Indian Bows & Arrows...The Old Way**/Wallentine	B00/18	$9.95
❑	**Making Arrows...The Old Way** by Doug Wallentine	B00/19	$4.00
❑	**Eagle's View Publishing Catalog of Books**	B00/99	$1.50

• •

At your local bookstore or use this handy form for ordering:

EAGLE'S VIEW PUBLISHING READERS SERVICE, DEPT ACE
6756 North Fork Road - Liberty, Utah 84310

Please send me the above title(s). I am enclosing $_____
(Please add $2.00 per order to cover shipping and handling.) Send check or money order - no cash or C.O.D.s please.

Ms./Mrs./Mr. _____

Address _____

City/State/Zip Code _____

Prices and availability subject to change without notice. Please allow three to four weeks for delivery.

THE TECHNIQUES OF NORTH AMERICAN INDIAN BEADWORK
by
Monte Smith

This exciting book contains directions for selecting, buying and using beaded materials; guidelines for either buying or making your own beadwork loom; and, an examination of Indian beadwork designs, their development, significance and uses.

With complete step-by-step instructions for all of the variations of beading techniques used in both loom and applique work, included are directions for beading round objects, rosettes and necklaces.

There are approximately 200 illustrations, examples and photos of beaded articles from 1835 to the present. Examples are from the Apache, Arapaho, Assiniboine, Bannock, Blackfoot, Cheyenne, Chippewa-Cree, Comanche, Cree, Crow, Flathead, Gros Ventre, Huron, Kiowa, Mohawk, Navajo, Ojibwa, Omaha, Otto, Piaute, Pottawatomi, Sac & Fox, Shoshone, Sioux, Umitilla, Ute, Winnebago and Yakima.

This is a book of 102 pages that anyone interested in Indian Beadwork will want to own and study.

NEW ADVENTURES IN BEADING EARRINGS
by
Laura Reid

This fantastic new book is fully illustrated and presents step-by-step instructions on making truly beautiful and distinctive earrings.

Written by noted craftsperson and author Laura Reid, each step is fully explained and the entire text has been "reader tested" and enthusiastically endorsed.

The styles include five-star, snowflake and cross point-style earrings; small fan, large bugle fan, large and small bugle fan, porcupine quill fan and circle fan-style earrings; and, three-square, bugle star in circle, large bugle rectangle, small bugle base, five bugle base, seven bugle base, ten bugle base and one dimensional cube square-type earrings.

All of the materials used are easily obtainable and all of the styles are based on seed beads and bugle beads. Further, from the styles explained and illustrated, and based on the easy-to-follow instructions, the reader is encouraged to go beyond the basics of the book and create their own designs.

Anyone who enjoys creating and then wearing beautiful craftwork will find this book to be a must.